TAKING STOCK

Protect Your Wealth and Create Reliable
Income for a Happy and Secure Retirement

TAKING STOCK

Protect Your Wealth and Create Reliable
Income for a Happy and Secure Retirement

By RYAN SKINNER

CelebrityPress®
Winter Park, Florida

DEDICATION

I dedicate this to all those people who are living in pain, whether due to addiction, poverty, or a struggle within. May you seek a connection with that which is great. Call it God, call it Source, call it whatever you want…just call on it from that quiet place within and know that IT will answer…

CONTENTS

CHAPTER 1

TAKING STOCK AND PAYING IT FORWARD

The minute I stepped into the reception area to greet Mr. and Mrs. Rocklin I could tell they were nervous. Mr. Rocklin shook my hand firmly, but averted his eyes slightly. His wife smiled briefly, began looking around as if she were sizing up everything about Summit Financial Partners, from the décor and furniture to the color of the wood used to build the front desk. I offered my usual big "Hello," but their responses, though genial, were a bit timid and guarded.

Like a lot of my clients, the Rocklins came to me upon referral. All I knew was that they were nearing retirement and that they weren't happy with their previous financial advisor. As is my custom during these initial "get to know" meetings, I did my best to put them at ease. As I led them into the spacious, thoroughly modern conference room, I offered them some ice water. Mr. Rocklin said sure, but Mrs. Rocklin said it wasn't necessary.

"I made it myself," I laughed, using a standard icebreaker. Sometimes that puts first time visitors at ease, but I noticed they were still looking at each other like they would rather be anyplace else. I used a hand motion to invite him to sit in the black swivel chair at the dark wood conference table where I meet all my prospective new clients. He sat and tapped nervously on the table; clutching the manila folder he was holding–presumably filled with elements of their financial history they had brought to have me review.

I walked to the other side of the table and pulled out the chair for Mrs. Rocklin. As she sat, I decided to break the ice and looked across at Mr. Rocklin, who was sizing up the room and straining to see what was outside the large glass window across from him. It was a few days after the Patriots won Super Bowl LI in the first overtime in Super Bowl history. I asked, "Are you guys Pats fans?" When you live in Woburn, which is 13 miles north of Boston, that's like saying, "Are you breathing?" Everyone's pretty much into the Pats and Tom Brady during football season, and the Red Sox in spring and summer. Surprisingly, it was Mrs. Rocklin who spoke first. "Comeback of the century," she said, referring to the Pats' comeback from a 28-9 deficit to the Atlanta Falcons. "Five-time Super Bowl champs. Probably the best team ever. No argument now."

"And Brady's 4th MVP," I said, referring to the legendary quarterback's new all-time record. "Unbelievable."

I continued talking about my longtime passion for the team and I could immediately detect a shift in their posture, facial expressions and overall demeanor. Assured they were in friendly territory and that I was there to help them, they loosened up and Mr. Rocklin loosened his grip on the folder and placed it on the glass tabletop. Everything felt more comfortable now and it was time to get down to business. I thanked them for coming in and reassured them that the purpose of this initial meeting was to see if I would be a good fit for their current and future financial needs.

The Rocklins are typical of many clients who come in nervously clutching their papers, concerned with such questions as: "Do we have enough? Is our money currently in the right places? And where do I begin pulling it from to build a retirement portfolio with you?" Even though they know I'm going to ask important questions about their current financial status and their long-term goals, they always bring doubts, anxieties and second thoughts before they're ready to take any major plunge.

I believe they are guarded because they're being asked to expose some very personal details to a person who, no matter how friendly or full of helpful, intentions, is essentially a stranger to them. It's probably similar to what doctors go through with new patients. Understandably, though I am probably the least judgmental person they will ever meet, they worry about being judged about the financial history they are expected to present. They might wonder, "What will he think if I tell him that we've been somewhat careless with our money, or if we tell him that we've managed to save hardly anything out of our monthly incomes so we don't have much to work with?" Maybe they have it in their heads that I only work with wealthy clients and they feel they wouldn't generate enough income for me to merit my investment of time.

Generally, there's a specific event–impending retirement, their children's college needs, a recent diagnosis that might necessitate long-term medical expenses–that brings people to that first meeting with me. That's often the first question I ask: "What brings you here today?" And if they're serious, I expect a meaningful straight answer and a willingness to share–even if they may feel a bit embarrassed at first–their current financial position in the form of assets, liabilities, spending patterns and their current income patterns. Once they get over their fears of sharing these details, the next logical step is finding out what their immediate and long-term goals are.

Many clients come to me because I have developed a strong reputation in my community as a retirement expert, but they still bring their previous experiences to that conference room table. I've met countless people, who became great clients, that have told me that they were initially skeptical of me simply because I work in an industry that they knew they needed to help them achieve their financial goals, but simply didn't trust.

Once I have gained their confidence and we have chosen to work together, they'll open up to me about some of their often shocking and appalling previous experiences with financial advisors. They'll tell me that their former advisors have lost them large sums of money, lied to them and not provided the quality service they promised. Even if they personally have not been burned, they'll tell me that that seeing illuminating films like "The Big Short" (about the financial industry greed that led to the housing bubble burst and the financial crisis of 2007-08) and hearing on the news the details about Bernie Madoff, who perpetuated the largest financial fraud in U.S. history, often color their perceptions of my industry–and make them hesitant about entrusting their life savings to anyone.

What they come to learn from spending more time with me is that while we at Summit Financial Partners are the ones who service them, their money is actually with institutions (not in our accounts) and our job is to guide them to the best companies and products to meet their needs and goals.

To help put prospective clients at ease, I take the time to address their specific concerns, identify with them and express the fact that I understand the reality that most advisors don't take the proper approach. I know we can only prove this by working with them over time, but we run our practice as if clients are family. We've created at Summit a very unique, nurturing, family environment that enables us to provide unparalleled individualized service for each of our clients. We work as a team to guide them in a direction that is best suited to meet their evolving needs and desires. Our business model is ultimately designed to protect the integrity of every client relationship.

Although it may seem strange to some, I proudly point out that I take a spiritual approach to my business, and happily explain why I feel it's appropriate–both personally and professionally– to do so. Some people are puzzled, others find it beautiful and inspiring. I just share this as honestly and openly as possible and leave their perceptions in God's hands. For years, I ran my business solely to make money and be considered successful and important, but after going through and ultimately surviving years of personal struggles and battles with addiction, I realized that I'm here to be of service. It's not just about the money, it's the journey and process that matter most. Likewise, it's not about any specific career goal or destination for me. I focus more on the person I am becoming over the course of my journey serving the needs of my clients.

In the case I mentioned about The Rocklins, they, like a lot of folks, had lost a great deal of their investment money in 2008 while working with an overly optimistic advisor that simply told them to "Stay the course" and "Ride out the storm." I pointed out to them that general financial advisors that are not retirement specialists are simply trying to do their best on behalf of the clients–but they're not suited to do retirement planning any more than a primary care physician is equipped to do open heart surgery.

MY MISSION

Stated simply, my mission as a retirement specialist is to be of service, to help people achieve an income for life–an income that lasts as long as they live, that always outpaces inflation and is sheltered from the great expenses of nursing home care. I sincerely want all of my clients to enjoy their retirement years to the fullest, whether that means enjoying maximum time with their children and grandchildren, traveling the world or cruising a few times a year, golfing or being free to pursue charitable or artistic endeavors they had put off for years because of work commitments.

If I had to formulate a literal mission statement, it would be based on two of my favorite quotes. The first is from Mahtatma Gandhi, who said, "The best way to find yourself is to lose yourself in the service of others." I'm always happiest and at my best when

I'm in with my clients, discussing strategies to help them achieve their goals. The moment I live for is when I enlighten them to a certain idea I have, or a product or combination of products I think will work for them, and I see their eyes light up and they smile lightly. That's how I know we're on the right track.

The second part of my mission statement would be the Biblical quote, "To whom much is given, much is expected." I'm by no means a Bible thumper, but that concept speaks loudly to me because at this point in my life, I feel beyond blessed. I wake up in a warm bed next to someone I love. I roll out of bed in the morning onto my knees, next to my bulldog whom I love, pray and ask that God allow me to be of service to others while using my talent, and then ask Him to handle the results.

Before heading to the office, I engage in the perfect routine, which gets me ready physically, mentally and spiritually for the day. I go and work out (another activity I love) and then meet for coffee with longtime friends who are more like brothers. We don't just chitchat; we discuss meaningful happenings and revelations in our lives and how we can grow into better men every day. Then I head off to a job I feel blessed by and spend my day with clients that are like family to me. After work, I return home, meditate and enjoy spending time with my wife and bulldog. It all sounds so simple, yet there's so much to be grateful for. I have been given so much, including a second chance at life and a better one than I could have ever imagined, especially considering where I was just a few short years ago. I am committed to paying it forward in any and every way I possibly can.

In reference specifically to my work with clients, a key part of my specific mission is taking the fear out of retirement planning by working with them closely and being transparent in every way. I believe that if you're honest, sincere and candid with people, the trust follows naturally, and that trust helps ease the fears they have about their future and their monthly income in retirement. My ultimate aim for every client relationship I have is that I provide peace of mind, so they can sleep without any worry about having enough money to live on and enjoy their lives with. My many years in the financial industry have taught me one essential truth: at the end of the day, all people want is someone who is honest and who genuinely cares.

To those who have not chosen it as a profession, the investment world can seem overwhelming and complex. Understanding this, I found a few important ways to help people understand where they are putting their money so that they can feel confident in my efforts on their behalf. Unlike most advisors, I don't move money in the first or second appointment. I walk clients steadily through the process of identifying what they need for income, maximizing their income from Social Security, identifying their income gap/shortfall, then introducing the solution to close that gap with guaranteed income for life. I include them in the details of the process every step of the way. In essence, they choose me and then I help them choose the money manager. Over the course of those meetings, the trust, relationship and usually a strong abiding friendship develops.

They understand that my team and I are there to preserve and protect their wealth so that they can have a secure and happy retirement. To accomplish this, we utilize tools that are fully insured with a portion of their money in order to ensure that their income gap is closed with an income that will never run out and will always keep up with inflation. To this end, there are guaranteed tools available that we, as retirement specialists, can gain access to.

MY INSPIRATION

My journey to becoming a financial advisor and retirement specialist started in 7th grade at Saint Agnes School in Arlington, Massachusetts with my teacher, Joan Morrissey, who knew I was dyslexic and had learning disabilities. She noticed that in spite of my shortcomings in other areas, I was skilled with numbers for my age. She introduced me to the stock market and to the legendary investor and philanthropist Peter Lynch, who was the manager of the Magellan Fund at Fidelity Investments between 1977 and 1990. His success story really inspired me. During his time managing that fund, he averaged a 29.2% annual return; during his tenure, assets under management increased from $18 million to $14 billion. I loved learning the details of the market and talking to Peter about his work in the industry. It was the first thing that ever made sense to me in my life–and I ran with it.

I'm passionate about what I do for a number of reasons. I get a huge rush out of seeing people get to enjoy their retirement. I wasn't raised in a wealthy family myself, so I love helping normal people have extraordinary retirements. The other driving force is the fact that for so many years, I can honestly say that I was a selfish person, a black hole when it came to empathy, compassion and true service. I made sure to help the clients because it was my job, but I was more concerned with myself, where I was traveling, what girl I was with at any given time, or the vehicle I was driving. My life was about Ryan, Ryan, Ryan.

After having major health issues, I realized that I wanted to find and live for something more–a purpose. And so now my purpose or "IT" is helping people, making a difference in their lives at my office and everywhere I can outside my professional environment. That includes the class I teach to recovering addicts who are inmates at the Middlesex House of Corrections in Billerica, and teaching kids at my alma mater, Arlington Catholic High School, to tap into their faith to help them with business and personal relationships. I explain how their relationship with God can strengthen their lives. Wherever I'm able to contribute my time and talents, it's all about being present and genuinely sincere.

The desire to live this way came from two distinctive phases in my life. When I was living in the hell that is being an addict, I would see people going to work, spending quality time with their families, playing a meaningful role in this world. Even back then, when I was self-destructive and self-absorbed, I knew that the only way out would be becoming "a part of something" important, contributing to the world, and playing a role, my role...

Earlier in my life, I remember watching my mom work as a housekeeper on my days off from school. I saw her on her hands and knees, scrubbing toilets and bathroom floors, smiling and singing. It didn't bother her, but it upset me that she would have to work hard at what I considered such a demeaning job. Looking back, my perspective on this was so wrong. I had no clue that I was watching someone who would someday be my hero. When I asked her how she was so happy when she should be upset–I had almost put her down because I was angry that she had to do that job–she would smile and call me by the nickname she always had for me, Ted. It's her nickname for me to this day because I always had my Teddy bear with me as a boy. (She works with me now and still calls me that even in front of clients!)

"Ted," she said, "I smile because I'm lucky enough to have work and take care of my kids. I'm going to make this the cleanest bathroom you'll ever see and give it my best. It's between me and God, not me and the people I work for. Always give everything you have and God will take care of you."

Who could have known then that the faith she had would eventually infiltrate my life and save me?

People often find it ironic when I tell them that being a drug addict was the best thing that could ever have happened to me. But they understand me better when I explain it to them this way. I say, "I had a terrible fall and thank God now that I can help people who are going through it." It gave me a purpose and a strong connection with divinity and my fellow human beings and in essence, made me bulletproof. When parents come to me feeling hopeless about their addicted child and tell me, "People don't recover," I tell them, "I recovered."

Looking back, I realize that I was a cancer in the lives of my parents, the children of my ex-wife and so many others–but now my only goal is to be a blessing to people. My day-to-day joy comes from being there for others, like so many were there for me. If one less mother can cry herself to sleep because of my story, I feel like everything I have been through was worth it. I'm blessed now and want to be a blessing to others.

Nothing I'm doing now would be remotely possible without falling to the lowest possible place and finding, with God's grace, a way out of that darkness. There's one particular moment that sparked me to take stock and realize that I was either going to die, or seek help to get out of my downward spiral, and make one final try to resume a respectable life.

I was being held in a jail cell in Cambridge, where I was able to look out and see my old office, the spot where I parked my nice car and go in and have clients introduced to me. I remembered it as an easy, soft life on the outside, but feeling like I was in hell on the inside. At that moment, I spoke out loud to a God that I wasn't sure existed, or if He did, I assumed that he wouldn't want anything to do with me. In that cell, I made the plea, "If You give me one more chance, I promise I won't drop the ball."

At that time, I didn't think I would get that shot, but I knew if I did, I would never give less than 100% to anyone or anything I was entrusted to. So that's what I give these days, at all times, from 4 a.m. when I start my morning prayers and do my meditation to hitting the gym at 5 a.m, having coffee with my friends at 6:15 a.m, my work with clients, friends and my wife. I give it all each day and lay it out there. Then at the end of each day, during my nightly prayer and meditation, I say, "God, I gave it all I had. I'm sure I came up short in some of those areas. Please take care of those. I hope I made you proud in some ways. Please handle the results. I know you didn't carry me this far to drop me on my head." Then I go to sleep immediately, unburdened, with a joyful, light heart.

I believe that every day, every success and blessing, and everything good in life is an unmerited gift from God. I just want to be of service and play a positive role in people's lives. I believe God works through people and that as human beings, we're either growing or retracting and going backwards. My choice is to grow. I aspire to do that each day to be the man God meant for me to be. So I try my best to give all of me to everyone I come in contact with. My business blesses me with the ability to have a deeply positive impact on people.

I was inspired to write *Taking Stock* because I am constantly asked by folks in my industry how I got to the level I am at. Although the ego inside me (which to me, stands for Edging God Out) wants to take credit for everything, the truth is that it comes from my deep connection with God. I don't believe that you can ask God for material things or personal success. However, I focus on paying it forward and God always partners up with me to ensure that I have enough success that I can bless others. The true measure of success is how many people you bless. That's just a fact of life.

The reason I'm writing this now is because we're living in a day and age where our world is being destroyed by opiates and addiction. Often, it seems hopeless and beyond redemption. I am hoping that my pain can bring hope to people by showing that addicts CAN and DO recover. I want people to know that we must not disregard people as "trash" and "junkies." Because if we give them a hand up (not a hand out) and help them rebuild their lives, they can be productive, tax paying members of society. We're alive at a time where we need hope and inspiration and we need to shine a light on the fact that the drug addict isn't some gross guy on the street who's just a thug or criminal. That person is a son, a daughter, a brother, a sister, and most devastatingly, a parent...It's me. And with love and concerted effort, we can save lives. It's possible, and it's very manageable, as long as love and God are at the center of it.

Now, onto business…

SEVEN WAYS YOU CAN TAKE STOCK OF YOUR RETIREMENT

I will be covering in depth seven basic areas of retirement planning throughout this book. Below, I provide a brief synopsis of each:

The Difference Between Saving for Retirement and Spending in Retirement

Saving for retirement is all about accumulation. You go to work and your money goes to work for you (via 401(k)s, IRAs, and so forth), slowly building up a nest egg. The advisor that services you during this phase is like a primary care physician whose job it is to help you keep your finances healthy. The main concern is ROI (return on investment), but, every seven to nine years on average, a stock market crash or economic storm wipes it out. When you're 15 years away from retirement, you can ride out the storm. But when you're in your 50s, you're entering the distribution phase. Now you're slowing down or not going to work anymore. At this point, your money needs to work twice as hard and twice as smart for you. It's time to turn that nest egg into income, and ROI changes its meaning into "Reliability of Income"–i.e. knowing you can pay for your food, clothing and shelter month in and month out. During the pre-retirement and retirement phase you can no longer afford to have any losses. We are retirement specialists, which is the medical equivalent of a cardiologist. Our job description is "asset preservation and wealth distribution specialist."

Essential Income and Discretionary Income: What You Need and What You Want

*Foundation: food, clothes, shelter

*Discretionary: fun money, i.e. travel, golf, helping grandchildren

How To Maximize Social Security, Pension and Other Retirement Income

We have a process to help clients maximize their Social Security utilizing switching strategies...When 90% of married couples, divorced individuals, widows and widowers go through the process, they received over $100k+ of additional income in retirement from the SS system. Well worth it!

How Annuities Can Provide a Secure, Guaranteed Long-Term Income

The right annuities can provide a client guaranteed income for as long as they live, including the ability to earn additional interest on years the market goes up, so the client participates in good years in the market, and principal protection, so the client NEVER incurs losses to their account.

The Importance of Disability and Long-Term Care Insurance

Having long-term care insurance, an annuity with a long-term care rider, or life insurance with a long-term care feature is very important. More and more people are living longer and needing care; products that offer these riders or protection give clients the ability to get care at a facility or at home.

How Life Insurance Can Provide Tax-free Benefits to Spouses and Children/Estate Planning and Asset Distribution–Your Legacy

Life insurance has many great features. A client can leverage these clients to get another source of income throughout retirement with no income taxes. It would be tax-free income if the client's advisor sets it up properly. Also, most solid life insurance products have a long-term care feature that enables a client to be properly protected without having to pay for long-term care insurance. Finally, life insurance products have a very strong death benefit that passes money tax-free to beneficiaries–which is an excellent way to pass money to one's children or a charity without having to pay taxes. This can be used to cover estate taxes, any debt that would be left behind, or simply leverage money a person wants to leave behind.

Before we begin the full on journey of *Taking Stock*, I just want to add one more thing that has truly motivated me to share my personal story and professional knowledge and wisdom here. I believe that when you go to your grave, they don't dump a Brink's truck into it. It's all about how many heads show up at your funeral. Meaning, when you're gone, when there's nothing more you can do for people, how many have you touched enough that they show up to pay their respects, expecting nothing in return.

I've been rich twice and poor twice, and I'll definitely take rich, but if all I am remembered for is how many dinners I buy or tabs I pick up, then I would consider my life a failure. I want to touch people and want them to know that I'm dedicated to helping those that can do nothing in return for me. I get my blessing and pay from God. I work for Him, and He pays me with the meaningful, enduring things that make life worth living: family, amazing friends, special clients, guys that are brothers and that genuinely love me (and I love them back!), and a happy, healthy relationship with a significant other. That's the good stuff.

Once you finish the book, I hope that you will understand what drives me and enables me to be on a level that most advisors and retirement specialists can only fathom. I want you to know why it seems like I really care about you on a level far deeper than dollars and cents; because I truly do.

CHAPTER 2

MONEY IS NEVER ENOUGH

When I say that I consider all of my clients like family, I truly mean it. I love creating special moments with them that brighten up my day and make my office seem as cozy and warm as a home environment. I always looked forward to my meetings with Fran and Maureen Greene. Fran was a special guy that I found particularly fascinating, a kind soul and a veteran with two Purple Hearts that he was happy to show me. The first time we ever met, he shook my hand firmly and pointed out what a weak handshake I had. He kept making me do it over and over again until I got it right. Now I greet all my new and longtime clients with the "Fran" handshake and I believe that it's helped me convey the kind of confidence that people are looking for in an advisor.

When Fran passed away in September 2016, I felt like I had lost a cherished buddy, but I felt blessed that Maureen, his beloved spouse of 33 years, was still in my life as a client and friend. I felt very close to her and wanted to do whatever it would take to keep her thriving financially and create a legacy for her husband. Maureen and I decided that since they had no children, we would set up a charitable trust that would donate money each year to vets in both of their names after she passes someday. They're great people and this was a great cause I was happy to set her up with.

My work on behalf of Fran and Maureen is just an example of helping people plan a special legacy. My clients are concerned about protecting their money from stock market loss and nursing home care, which are the two greatest offenders to a healthy, happy retirement. But, they also want to ensure, that when all is said and done, their money goes to their kids, loved ones or charities in the most efficient manner possible–and not the nursing home or the state of Massachusetts.

There are many ways to create a legacy. Some people want to make sure their grandkids get an education. Some want to leave their kids money. Others have disabled children and for them we need to set up certain trusts to ensure that the kids don't receive a windfall of money and lose their benefits. Many of my clients, like me, are truly grateful to the Veterans like Fran, those men and women that sacrificed their lives so that we can live free in this great country–so they set up charities to leave money behind to help these folks. Many of us who have been touched by addiction want to leave money to help men and women struggling to get help and recover so that they too can be the parents, sons, daughters, brothers, sisters and productive members of society that they are meant to be.

I always like to say that it's not about the money, but what we use it for. If we get clients great returns one year but they're in risky products, then we didn't truly give them anything of value because they could lose it the next year. Those kinds of paper gains, i.e. mutual funds and stocks and bonds, are by definition not solid. On the other hand, when we utilize tools that insure our clients' principal and lock in all gains, we give our clients solid, enduring gains that enable them to enjoy their retirement years with greater peace of mind.

LEARNING THE REAL VALUE OF MONEY

Back in my 20s, I really didn't understand the truth about the value of money and the best ways to use it. I made a great income, but I was using it to try and fill a hole within myself rather than having a big picture perspective about how I (and the money) could be of benefit to others. I was all about me, me, me in those days. I bought watches, clothes and cars and put a great emphasis on consumerism and accumulating "stuff." I tried traveling, and it was the same result. I also entered into friendships and romantic relationships selfishly in one-sided attempts to fill a void inside. I dated more girls and lived the wrong way, only to find that girls didn't fill the emptiness, either. Even got married thinking that would help, but it didn't. During this time in my life, I started trying to fill that void with drugs and alcohol. They were a solution that worked for a while, but then as it took more and more to keep me "up," it started to not work so well. Then it didn't work at all, and I was left a broken man–poor, lonely, addicted, lost and with no connection to God. My spirit was lost. Ultimately, I paid a huge price to learn the truth. You can't fill a God-size hole with stuff. Or drugs.

I remember during this time I was working for myself, but every day I felt that hole inside me grow bigger and bigger. Work would go well, but I had very few hobbies. My day to day was work, girls, the gym and going out for dinner and drinks. This industry can be up and down. The roller coaster was rough and still is. But with spirituality, God and meditation, I stay balanced because I know for a fact that there is a loving energy/Source, which I choose to call God that always provides for me. As long as I live right, I believe things will always be moving in a positive direction. The most concrete fact I have is the existence of God in my life.

These days, on the blissful other side of a harrowing journey into and slow burn out of a hell of multiple addictions, I feel like I'm living proof that with deep faith, the encouragement of loving friends, sponsors, mentors and family and an effective 12-step program, anything is possible. I am truly dedicated to taking advantage of my second chance at life. I am building a successful business and paying my reversal of fortune forward in many fulfilling ways. These days, I use my money to donate to those in need, help others and engage in thoughtful and kind actions rather than selfish/self-seeking activities whose only goal is self-gratification. I try to use my blessings to be a blessing to others.

MY DESCENT INTO ADDICTION

Like a lot of addicts, my descent into heavier addictions began with those few extra stress-relieving drinks at lunch and after work that developed into alcoholism. At the time, the outside world might have looked at me like things were going great. After I graduated with a degree in finance from Merrimack College, I got a job as a broker dealer with a renowned investment firm. Within a few years, I had launched my own successful firm focused on retirement planning. I was what you might call a "functioning alcoholic." I served my clients well and gave them peace of mind with the money they'd worked their whole lives for. However, inside my soul was dying. The more money I made, the more I drank. Then I got into pills. In my early to mid-20s, I had hand surgery and developed a small addiction to Percocet. Things got out of hand quickly over the years.

When I was 27, I developed a painful esophagus condition known as the Mallory-Weiss tear. This occurs in the mucus membrane of the lower part of the esophagus or upper part of the stomach, near where they join. I think it was due in part to my job related stress and increased drinking. I bled out and was in a coma for a time, and a stomach surgery was performed to save my life. Coping with the pain led to more addictive behavior. I went from one 5 mg of Percocet per day to five, 10 and 15 pills. I then switched to the heavier Oxycotin, peaking at 20 crushed 80 mg pills per day snorted up my nose. Just to give you an idea, 1,600 mg of Oxycotin is equivalent in strength to 320 Percocet pills. My painkiller habit escalated to a full-blown heroin addiction. That's when I say the lights went out. I lived in my condo, which was in foreclosure, with no electricity or TV. Often I would find myself in drug houses in rough areas of Massachusetts for days on end because I had no way to get home or get around. I lost everything–my house, car, retirement, clothes, watches, business, office, the ability to provide for myself, and more importantly, the respect of my family, friends and two beautiful stepsons. I went from making half a million dollars a year to essentially being homeless. Everything I had worked hard for was gone. Perhaps the most crucial thing I lost was my relationship with God, that Source that's inside that guides us, gives us that spark of life, a soul, a spirit, joy, everything. I truly lost my soul.

I like to think that God sometimes allows us to hit rock bottom so that His strength can take over and help us climb out–but only, of course, when we recognize our need for his help, love and mercy. My rock bottom was truly unfathomable. I began waking up in dirty places, smoking used cigarettes I found on the ground and hitting the streets shaking a cup for money to buy more dope. Over the course of a few years, I had some stupid arrests for assault and battery and resisting arrest. I overdosed at least eight times. At one point, I tried to commit suicide by mixing heroin with Klonopin. My plan was to OD and get thrown outside a detox center with a suicide note, so my parents wouldn't be the ones to find me dead. But then it was like God said, "Enough, Ryan!" and intervened. An ambulance happened to be pulling up at that moment. The EMTs gave me two shots of Narcan and saved my life. I'm grateful God had other plans for me. I can't imagine how awful it would have been to face Him in death in the shape I was in.

You would think having my life saved would have woken me up, but I was so messed up that it took a little longer. Not long after that episode, I was arrested for another street scuffle I'd gotten into. One of the probation officers, familiar with my history, actually said, "You're a great guy, Ryan, but we give you so much rope and you always hang yourself with it."

I alluded to this moment in Chapter One. I'm certain now that

God in his wisdom had them place me in that certain holding cell for a reason, so that I could look out and "see" my former life and make some heartbreaking comparisons. I felt very defeated, sad that I had squandered the opportunities I had. Yet, in some ways, I felt I was no freer then. Then it happened. It was like God was no longer just operating behind the scenes, getting me to this moment. I felt His presence in that cell. The spirit came over me and without even realizing what was coming out of my mouth, I found myself pleading, "If you give me one more shot, I will NEVER make those same mistakes again." I felt like if somehow I was able to come back from this, what an epic comeback story it would be. I'd be able to help a ton of people.

MY ROAD TO REDEMPTION AND GRATITUDE FOR THOSE RESPONSIBLE

I often describe the recovery process as something that happened over a long period of time, yet all of a sudden. See, I had been to a 12-Step program before, but hadn't truly committed. Enrolling is easy; doing the actual work is hard. Maybe the point is that I had to, as they say, "Let go and let God." I couldn't do any of this on my own power. It was God who helped me commit to the 12-Step that brought me out of the darkness. I had no choice. Death was the only other option, but I know God never gives up on us; it's the prodigal son thing. I believe God knew my thoughts, that nobody who knows the pain would choose it. Nobody wants to be dirty, grimy, hungry and dope-sick all the time. That's the worst feeling in the world. I would wake up (if you can call it that) and lay in bed moving around, feet kicking, muscles twitching and it felt like my spine was vibrating. My bones hurt, and I was freezing and shaking, yet sweating profusely, stomach in cramps, always feeling like I had to throw up.

While most of my former friends had abandoned me when I went to jail, I was blessed to find new friends committed to helping me take the long road out of addiction. I had heard the expression, "It takes a village," but never knew what it meant until I experienced the love and support of a virtual village of kindhearted folks around me, extending much more kindness than I had ever given to anyone in my life. In many ways, I felt unworthy but to this day I am so grateful for everything they did to help. I intend to spend my life paying them back and, as I've said before, paying it forward to bless others. The reason I am alive and successful is directly due to God working through these incredible people.

My sponsor, Billy T, played a key role. He adopted me, put his hand out, visited me in jail, and loved me. He brought me lunch when I was home, dirty and poor. He called to check in on my mom, who was a complete stranger to him, and listened to her cry. Eventually, he took me through the steps and put my hand in the hand of God. I feel that he was put in my life because he was a successful professional who had once been where I was. He was the type of man I wanted to be, and he taught me how to live.

With his help, I began taking stock of who I was—an insecure guy with a lot of fears who would compensate by overachieving at work and at the gym. I had fears of not getting what I wanted and losing what I had. The fears fueled the addiction. Now, looking back, I realize they are my strength, because the fear of failure drives me to be successful in my business. To this day, Billy plays a profound role in all areas of my life. He taught me how to make God my business partner and bring God/spirituality into my day-to-day business, so that I could truly be of service to my clients.

After coming to terms with these insecurities and fears, I reconnected with some of my former clients, making amends. I assured them that while I never stole money from them, I know I stole their peace of mind through my addiction-fueled scattered attentiveness. Some came back, others didn't, but with the help of another mentor, Brian Donahue, I was able to get back on my feet. I launched my firm Summit Financial Partners and got on the road to building a new business. Brian was an established financial industry professional I had long revered. He had been a mentor to me when I was younger. He returned to help coach me back to mainstream life. He is a part of the reason that we are able to provide our clients with such great products and strategies and always put the clients first. The key to this relationship was that Brian always told me the truth.

Another key person in my recovery was Vinny Piro, Chief of Probation for the Woburn District Court, who put an end to my drug use and the hell I was in. He helped me get into the program "Reflections" that enabled me to rebuild my life, and then continued to guide me on every level. I once considered Vinny a feared nemesis, but he later became my close friend. I am always popping by his office for some java and conversation. As a friend, he gives me some honest feedback, whether it's relationship advice, business advice or guidance to help others with addiction. Vinny, along with Mike Higgins, started an important regional education and treatment initiative called the Heroin Education Awareness Task (HEAT) program. Their mission is to educate the state about heroin and try to stop this vicious epidemic. Mike was my probation officer, and although we got into heated arguments that were often very aggressive, they made decisions for me that I was not able to make for myself.

Not all addicts in recovery are as blessed as I am with the support of their families. I consider my sister a good friend. It's beautiful watching her take such great care of my grandparents as they near the end of their lives. She's kind, gentle and makes them light up when she walks in the room. I couldn't be prouder of her. My father is the kind of man of whom I can say, "If I turn out to be half the man my dad is, I'll consider myself a huge success." He taught me that a real man is faithful to his wife, provides for his family, lives honestly and sincerely and has integrity. I was really blessed with an awesome role model in him.

My best friends David and Shawn, who were brought up as foster brothers, have always been there for me. David is there for me as a positive role model, kind and honest. He overcame a hellish upbringing but got involved in union politics and was active back in school. Shawn is another loving guy, an amazing buddy and great dad. Then there's Dan, a nice young man that I sponsored who has grown to be a real quality man and helps me run the jail program. He also helped me get involved in the practice of stoicism and is deeply dialed into the spirit of mindfulness.

There are so many more folks in this village of support, but I will just mention a few more. I saw Ed Bleu for court ordered anger management and relapse prevention before going to jail. He runs a pod at the jail, and now has me and Dan, who's like my little brother, go in and "run the obstacles" as a group, enabling us to help and touch others. Kevin Meaney was the Assistant Chief of Probation in Woburn. Even when I was at my lowest point, he always treated me like a man, looked me in the eye and shook my hand. He is now a chief in Natick–a much-deserved promotion for a great guy.

Dr. Peltz is another person I have long valued. He is the psychiatrist who treated me even when I couldn't pay him. He allowed me to run a tab, trusting and betting that I'd be one of the fortunate ones to recover. He made a smart bet. He has helped me work on medication, staying grounded and mindfulness–all of which enable me to be present with a client and try to help them achieve their goals, and also work with addicts and alcoholics to try to help them rebuild their lives. Another important medical professional in my life is Scott Carpenter, who was my therapist who first introduced me to a 12-step program. He also allowed me to have sessions with him and run a tab when I was getting back on my feet. He helped me learn to practice self-love and be kind and forgiving to myself.

Finally, there is Steve Biagioni, who was the principal of my alma mater, Arlington Catholic High School. He took the lead in enabling me to start working with students regarding drug and alcohol issues. Together we have done everything from seminars and group talks with students and parents to having me run classes. Steve is a special person and I've grown immensely from his enduring friendship.

MY COMMITMENT TO GIVING BACK

Thanks in part to all of those folks I have mentioned who have gone above and beyond for me, my faith in God and my commitment to a future that is much different than my past. I am a new and better person. Professionally and personally, my life now is one of honesty and integrity, a daily dedication to living the right way, being kind and loving to others, taking a person who nobody could tolerate and being kind to that person.

I like to say I had to fall to gain it all. I grew up with a father and grandfather who taught me the value of integrity and I had to lose everything to gain that sort of integrity and live my life according to what I learned so many years ago. I broke my parents' heart once and now to see their joy in the life I lead is everything to me. I sponsor recovering addicts and when I see the light go on, and I can take that kid who was once on the couch half dead and show him how to live right, that's what's important to me. Making a difference in people's lives is what drives me every day. It's like a ripple effect. If you do the right thing, you can't help but make someone else's life better.

People who know me personally often hear me say, "What was once my curse is now my blessing." What I mean by this is that from my pain and the hell I went through came my "it." Each person has an "it," the one thing they were meant to be and do. My "it" isn't what I earn, drive, where I live or who's around me. As a retirement specialist, my "it" is to help seniors achieve safe, guaranteed income solutions. On a personal level, my "it" is helping addicts find hope and build amazing lives that they love so much that they wouldn't consider sacrificing or squandering it for the momentary high of a drug. My "it" also involves helping parents and children of addicts to deal with their pain. I believe my purpose is to make the lives of other people better, and I am at my happiest when I'm being of service to others.

I believe in the old adage about putting your money where your mouth is. A lot of recoverees talk big about what they're going to do with their second chances at life, but then they just get caught up in the day to day and never act upon their stated ambitions. To me, gratitude is an action word. I take my commitment to serve others in the wake of my recovery very seriously. There's a saying in the Bible that I like, "To whomever much is given, of him much will be required, and to whom much was entrusted, of him more will be asked." I literally prayed for guidance to fulfill this in my own life and I felt that God opened the doors to many wonderful opportunities.

In 2014, I began working with Arlington Catholic, teaching kids to tap into their faith to help them with business and personal relationships, and explaining how their relationships with God can strengthen their lives. I continue to teach weekly classes there, using different spiritual readings to help them build the lives they want to live. I talk about how I was once in their seats, how I fell into hell and how God gave me another shot. I talk about how God isn't in the sky, but a more intimate presence in our lives, and that we have a GPS (God Positioning System/God Guidance System) that lives in us and can guide us to make good decisions and enjoy a great life. If we listen to that inner voice, we will have lives with less chaos and negativity. In addition to becoming a sponsor myself to younger recovering addicts, I speak at other high schools throughout my home region.

In 2015, I began speaking regularly at the Middlesex House of Corrections in Billerica, talking to inmates enrolled in the drug program there about making positive changes and turning adversity into positives. I teach a ten-week class devoted to helping people overcome their obstacles in the hopes of motivating them to recover from their addictions and rebuild their lives. I base my teachings on a popular book called *The Obstacle Is the Way: The Timeless Art of Turning Trials into Triumph* by Ryan Holiday. In addition to conducting my Friday morning class, I also meet one on one with many of the guys there in recovery one additional day during the week. In this setting, I talk about overcoming obstacles, building character, growing a positive attitude, having grit and resilience, blasting through obstacles, becoming men of integrity and accountability and becoming solid fathers and spouses. I make sure they remember that when you're pointing the finger at someone, there are always three fingers pointing back.

I have developed tremendous relationships with the inmates I meet there. I am especially close with Jimmy, a 34-year-old man who is like a younger brother to me now. He has spent the majority of his life in the Department of Youth Services, then jails and prisons. To say the least, he was a career inmate who had lost his son, his freedom and his life. He has had a tough existence and nobody thought he could or would ever change. Ed Bleu runs the block that Jimmy is on in jail. He believes people aren't addicts or thugs, but troubled human beings. Ed gave me a great gift by putting Jimmy in my group. It took a few weeks, but I watched the lights come on in Jimmy's eyes. Over time, I watched him grow, take accountability and literally change his moral fiber. I would make suggestions to him like meditation, praying on his knees and journaling to God–an activity that many in jail think is a sign of weakness. Although he was reluctant at first, Jimmy took every suggestion I gave him and he has really taken off. When he was denied parole, I feared he might slip backwards or fall off the wagon, but his response was quite the opposite. He showed me the man he is today, telling me, "God must think I have more work to do here." Jimmy is the go-to guy on the block now. People ask him for advice regarding spirituality, decisions they need to make regarding conflicts and the pain of missing their families. We recently started a new group for our program and asked Jimmy to go through it as a peer leader. He is doing an amazing job!

Also in 2015, I had the opportunity to serve as the guest speaker at a conference hosted by the HEAT Force Program. I focus these talks on making changes and turning adversity into something positive. Doing this, I have learned that the true measure of success is found in how many people you bless through the grace of God. I have also had the opportunity to get involved with that town's social services organization, the Council of Social Concern. I am fortunate enough to be able to regularly donate gift cards to Walmart and Market Basket as well as donate clothes and gifts around the holidays to needy families so their kids can have a nicer Christmas. I would drop them off personally to people. I continue to donate regularly to the council, Arlington Catholic and St. Patrick's Parish in Stoneham.

This past year, I also started a small organization called The Ryan Fund, which is dedicated to raising money for children who have been orphaned by parents who lost their struggle with addictions and veterans who are battling those destructive demons. This fund is an extension of my mission to be of service and to show people that despite the great odds, there is always hope. The catalyst for starting The Ryan Fund was a photo in the Boston Herald in May 2015 of a 10-year-old girl who had lost her parents to overdoses two weeks apart. I was immediately motivated to act. I called the foster care where she lived and inquired about adopting her. Because of my background with addictions, they wouldn't let me apply. However, I still wanted to give this girl and others like her a better life. I decided to help veterans as well because they are our heroes who fought for our freedom and the system is letting so many of them down. We are currently trying to get The Ryan Fund off the ground with various fundraising efforts.

THE TAKEAWAYS AND MY ROAD FORWARD

I'm the first to admit that recovery is a lifelong process, but I'm grateful to God that I can now share the harrowing story with a happy ending. A few years ago, it easily could have ended in tragedy. I hang out sometimes with other friends who also made it out–husbands, fathers, business owners and employees. We get together weekly in a group my sponsor, Billy, and I began hosting in my living room. We call our group "Dead Men on Vacation (DMOV)," because, based on how we lived and what we did to ourselves as addicts, we should all be dead. We're all grateful for second chances, and for the grace and mercy of God. We've all dedicated our lives to giving back.

Along the way, I learned that in the end, our relationships are all that matters–how we treat people, how we impact their lives. That's our legacy and it's what defines us as human beings. And I firmly believe that when this life is over, it's that which God judges us on and ultimately what creates our destiny.

All of these realizations play out day to day in the way I treat my clients. It's all about them. The old Ryan would do a great job for them, but I would be focused more on the commission I was about to make. These days I couldn't tell you what I make each week. I really don't care because I work for the Big Guy. As long as I give my all to my clients, and help people in pain whether they're addicts, poor or someone I pass on the street who simply looks sad or hungry, I know God will continue to bless me.

In fact, once I realized that God would provide for me the same way he provides for the grass, the birds and nature as a whole, I knew that all I needed to do was live the way He created me to live and simply put people first. As a result I have many thriving client relationships. I never take on clients that I don't click with, so I go to work every day to service people that I genuinely like. That is such a great gift.

Another phrase I like to say is, "It's not about the destination, it's about who you become on the journey." In other words, there's really no finish line. I used to think that everything was about "the goal." It's more about how you deal with the obstacles thrown at you, how you handle adversity and how you treat people who can't do anything for you. It's about developing character and grit, and growing closer to God naturally. For me, the focus is on growing into the man God intended me to be. I'm not quite there yet, but I'm sure as hell not the guy I once was. I think we're all works in progress.

When I start working with new clients, my questions for them are all pretty similar. I want to know what and who are important to them. Do they dream of traveling in their retirement, more time visiting their grandchildren, playing golf or leaving a legacy for their kids or their community? And what is their monthly income need for essentials like food, clothes, shelter and medical? I talk to them like people and develop a rapport with colorful conversation. I don't immediately start taking notes. I talk to them about weather, sports, kids and grandkids and even let them in on my own situation with my wife, friends and clients.

The most exciting aspect of my work is that there is no "cookie cutter" retirement strategy. Their needs are unique based on things like their age, whether this is their first marriage or they have been married multiple times, how many kids they have and how many of them are still dependents and if any of them are disabled. Everyone has different specifics related to their 401(k) s, IRAs, pensions, Social Security, savings and CDs, brokerage accounts, life insurance, rental properties, home mortgage balances and personal debt.

Everyone is different and I care about my clients as individuals. I make sure that comes across from the moment I meet them for the first time in the reception area. I'm here for you, I tell them. How can I be of service and give you a secure future?

CHAPTER 3

THE TWO ROIs

Even though all of my training in the finance industry is related to the nuts and bolts of my role as a retirement specialist, sometimes I feel that those initial meetings across the glass table find me playing the role of a therapist or psychologist. Everything I say in that initial conversation has to be sensitive, conveying compassion for what they've been through and concern for their current welfare. I have to realize that these people coming to meet me have been burnt before either by bad advisors or stock market storms. They are often hurting and skeptical so I make sure to listen attentively and ultimately steer the conversation out of the gloom and doom and into more hopeful visions–which I then work hard to turn into effective, detailed strategies.

I was all smiles with chatty small talk when Mrs. Grossman entered the conference room, but she looked like the weight of the world was on her shoulders, and she only made incidental eye contact with me as she gave me a weak, perfunctory handshake. I offered her a seat and she kept looking out the window and barely touched her water. I knew she wasn't in the mood for sports or pop culture so I got down to business, thanked her for coming in and asked, "What brings you here today?" I knew she would be one of those potential clients I'd most want to help. She didn't have to utter a word and somehow I knew the basics of her story. She fidgeted a bit, pulling up the sleeves of her black sweater and it took her a few minutes to open up. Her eyes were watery and

I could tell there was some pain she was still dealing with that went beyond just financial burden.

"My husband died five years ago and left me what I thought would be a great nest egg that would complement my Social Security and his ongoing pension payments," she said. "But I let him handle the investments over the years and never really discussed those things with him. So I didn't know who to go to in order to invest this money. I guess I should have known better than to have listened to a so called friend of a friend, but that's where I got the name of the guy who lost me a lot of the money my husband left me to care for. My grown son and daughter live down in New York, and they told me to do further research but I just wanted to get things done so I didn't have to worry about them."

"I'm sorry to hear about your husband and I'm sure all of this was difficult for you to handle," I said. "I know it's not easy to make decisions after we suffer a great loss."

Mrs. Grossman thanked me and seemed to feel more comfortable in sharing more of her story. Basically, in a rash of risky investments, her previous so called "retirement guy" made her suffer some serious losses. She realized that if she didn't get off the elevator where it was now, she might be riding it into the basement. She had never heard the term ROI (Reliability of Income) before, but I explained that this is a concept folks in my business use when we're talking about the best way to ensure that our clients can enjoy the best return on their investments and keep an income stream flowing throughout their retirement.

Once I had the basics of her troubling narrative, I knew a sure way to restore the twinkle to her eyes and add just enough hope for her to walk out of the conference room feeling that all was not lost. I told her about Fixed Indexed Annuities, something I will go into much greater detail about later in this book. I told her that for hundreds of my clients, they were wonderful supplements to their monthly Social Security and pension payments.

Once we studied the details of her accounts, Mrs. Grossman was happy to realize that she had just enough money to invest in what some people call "sleep assurance" investments. It took her a while to understand the math I slowly presented her with, but she felt assured that I was on her side after having the terrible experience with someone in my field who definitely was not. When she told me that her previous "adviser" had never mentioned annuities, I knew that we were on the road to daylight, and it was a delight to educate her. Once she got more involved in the strategies I presented to her, she beamed with pride and said, "My husband must be looking down, laughing and smiling that I know so much about these things now." I told her it was my pleasure to share my expertise with her, but more importantly, that I could provide her the kind of peace of mind she deserved.

Long story short, by bringing her assets to me and switching to a fixed indexed annuity, Mrs. Grossman ensured that whatever money she had remaining would never go down and would only go up from there. By getting her into the right products, I helped protect her remaining principal and ensured that she would lock in any and all gains. On a personal level, it felt good to have played an important role in turning her life from one of fear and despair to one of assurance and hope.

The biggest positive for good folks who come to me, like Mrs. Grossman, are that despite some major setbacks they usually still have a decent amount of money to work with. So they come to a retirement specialist like me who can protect their money from stock market loss and/or nursing home care and build an income for life. As I've said before, it's not always easy to win them over because of past bad experiences, so it's important to not only show kindness and understanding, but also showcase solid mathematics and previous client success stories. Every person has a unique life and experiences to share, but all of them come to me with similar fears and goals. Regardless of how much money they are starting with, their three greatest questions are: Do I have enough? Is it in the right places? What's the most efficient manner in which to pull down retirement income?

It may seem obvious, but one of the most important things I tell potential clients is that they can't turn back time, and nothing good comes out of dwelling on the negatives of the past. Then comes the good news: they're here now and I can help them move forward in confidence. We can learn from our past, then we must realize it's time to move on. I have learned this many times in my personal life as well. One of my favorite expressions is, "It's a good idea to look in the rear view on occasion so you don't make the same mistakes again, but if you stare too long, you'll go off the tracks."

In order to get them back on track, I gather information to determine what investment tool will best protect their money and fit their situation and goals. I believe that the first ROI works best when people are young, because later on in life, a few stock market storms can literally wipe people out. From my many years of experiences in this business, I believe that Return on Investment is the thing that matters most for pre-retirees and retirees.

THE FIRST ROI

Generally speaking, when I say ROI (Return on Investment), I'm talking about the benefit to an investor resulting from an investment of some resource. A high ROI means the investment gains compare favorably to the original cost of the investment. As a performance measure, ROI is used to evaluate the efficiency of an investment or to compare the efficiency of a number of different ones. To calculate ROI, the benefit (or return) of an investment is divided by the cost of the investment, and the result is expressed as a percentage or a ratio.

So, ROI = Gain from Investment - Cost of Investment ÷ by the Cost of the Investment. In this formula, "gain from investment" refers to the proceeds obtained from the sale of the investment of interest. Because we measure ROI as a percentage, we can compare it easily with returns from other investments, allowing us to measure investments against each other. ROI is a popular metric for many people because it's so simple and versatile, and it's a basic way to gauge an investment's profitability. Think of it this way: if you are presented with an investment and you learn it does not have a positive ROI, or if you learn about others who have a more positive ROI, these values can be compared to help people naturally choose the one with the higher rate of return.

The "accumulation phase" is the phase of the investor's life when he or she builds up his or her savings and the value of his or her investment portfolio with the intention of having a nest egg for retirement. By choosing to defer spending until later in life, individuals create savings that can be invested in the marketplace and grow over time. Assuming that people periodically invest money over the duration of their working lives, individuals can create a long accumulation period during which their savings can grow substantially. When people are working and planning for their retirement, they generally focus on getting the highest Return on Investment for their money.

I call this "The First ROI."

Return on Investment is important during the accumulation phase (ages 30-55) because that's when you're trying to build your nest egg, save as much as possible and during those years is when you have time to rebound from stock market crashes and corrections that happen on average every seven to nine years. When you still have ten years to go before your retirement, you can easily come back from a crash–even ones as bad as those in the early 2000s and the one that led to The Great Recession in 2007-2008. The closer a person gets to retirement, the harder it is to recover. I had a guy come to me in 2007 who planned to stop working in 2010. To put it mildly, he didn't do the right planning. In 2008, his 401(k) became a "201(k)" and it was too little, too late. He's still working to this day, which to me is a very sad thing. Watching this kind of unexpected turn of events happen motivates me to help as many clients as I can to avoid them.

In the building (accumulation) phase of investing, the benefits of using stocks and mutual funds in investment accounts are that there's always more upside potential, but this is balanced by greater risk because these investments are subject to daily shifts and general trends on the market. During this phase, you go to work and your money goes to work for you in 401(k)s, IRAs and things of that nature.

Certain instruments like those 401(k)s, IRAs and other qualified retirement accounts require that you pull money out after you reach a certain age, no matter what the market conditions are. With IRAs, Uncle Sam lets you grow your money for years–but with a catch. I say that a deferred IRA is an IOU to the IRS. All of those investments follow the same rules and regulations. But then when you're 70 and a half, they want their taxes so they devised what's called a Required Minimum Distribution (RMD). You generally have to start taking withdrawals at this age from your IRA, SIMPLE IRA, SEP IRA, 403(b) or retirement plan account. Your RMD is the minimum amount you must withdraw from your account each year. If a client should for some reason lose money the same year they are required to start their RMD, they usually don't recover. This is another reason why it's crucial to set up a retirement plan of guaranteed income that is not subject to loss.

When you're trying to build your nest egg, the advisor helping call the shots is like a primary care physician. We focus on the distribution phase, where we turn that nest egg you accumulated into income. As a retirement specialist, I'm the equivalent of a cardiologist. I help clients take that nest egg and protect it from stock market loss and/or nursing home care–then ensure that my clients get an income for life. Our niche is in helping clients nearing or currently in their retirement to build income for life, creating for them a guaranteed income stream that lasts as long as they live and always keeps up with inflation–and that is also sheltered from nursing home care.

THE SECOND ROI

People approaching retirement age, from age 55 upward, should shift their focus as soon as possible to what I call "The Second ROI," which I call "Reliability of Income." This simply means protection of your nest egg, it's knowing that your money is safe and that you'll have guaranteed income month after month, year after year, for as long as you live regardless of what goes on in the stock market. In this phase of your life, you don't have as much time to recover from severe corrections in the market. This is where my company, Summit Financial Partners, shines.

There are several key reasons why I've chosen to deal exclusively with people aged 54-75 and help them manage their nest eggs—and not with younger investors in different phases of their investment lives. First, growing up, I felt that my parents were the hardest working people I knew, and I had a big extended family with a powerful work ethic that I respected so much. Let's just say that they were not aristocrats. So when I was getting into the financial industry, a lot of them were getting towards retirement age and needed answers to know that the money they had accumulated would be taken care of. It made sense to me to make my own career about being of service to people I cared about. My loved ones were freaking out about a lot of issues related to their retirement, but when I gave them the answers they were looking for, they started smiling. The other reason I like dealing with people of retirement age is the value system that's part of their generation. I find them more straightforward and appreciative than younger folks. Little things like eye contact, humility and the natural ability to shake hands as a gesture of good faith go a long way with me.

Once my clients know it's time to make the switch from the first ROI to the second ROI I explain to them that it's no longer about how big their accounts are, dollar or size wise. Rather, what matters now is the size of their guaranteed income. I've heard it said that baby boomers all have egos because their greatest concern is the size of their accounts. It's my opinion, however, that ego stems from insecurity and the reality is that they're the children of parents who lived through The Great Depression in the 1930s, so most likely the fear was built into them from the time they were very young.

I can offer a strong example of the way I helped a client make a smooth transition at this "shift point." Remember, I mentioned Maureen and Fran at the beginning of Chapter 2. When I first started working with Maureen, she had all her money in either the bank or a 401(k). I sat with her and addressed the positive aspects about protecting her retirement, ensuring that she and her husband, Fran, would have income for life. These folks were not greedy; instead they were sensible and coachable. I am happy to say the majority of people who become cherished clients are like them. I think most coming into the distribution phase have the common sense these days to protect their nest egg.

Everyone remembers 2001-2003 and only a fool could forget 2008. Every so often someone will point out that they could be giving up some interest on years the market goes big. I explain that I once heard the expression that goes, "You give a little to get a little." But happily, that's not the case with the retirement strategies I create with the products I use. At Summit Financial Partners, I always say, "You give a little to get a lot." You can ask my clients how grateful they were in 2008 when their neighbors lost 38% of their assets while they lost absolutely nothing. All of that is due to smart retirement investing during the Reliability of Income phase.

COSTS AND INCOME STREAMS IN RETIREMENT

In planning "The Second ROI" phase of retirement, we first must consider the basics–i.e. the costs of being retired and how much money people need to meet their monthly expenses. Important issues to consider are taxes, long-term care and health care, and their basic living expenses, mortgages and rent, utilities, food–all the things they had to think about when they were in the workforce.

Let's start with taxes. They are different in each state, relative to that state's laws and regulations. Long-term care and health care costs, on the other hand, are universally massive and because of the expense, I am not a fan of long-term care insurance. In working with clients, I prefer to use a hybrid life insurance product that offers tax-free income, a death benefit, and long-term care coverage without extra expenses. Also, I utilize annuities that have long-term care riders to help pay for care.

As for living expenses, these are the details I talk about regularly at workshops that I host for people–both clients and non-clients– up to four nights a month. We do a Social Security workshop that focuses on how to maximize a person's Social Security, identify "income gaps" and explains how to close those monthly/yearly gaps with guaranteed income for life. The other one is what we call "Creating a Retirement State of Mind," in which we discuss how we help people transition from building and growing to preserving and taking income. That's where people who are not yet clients get to know me and what Summit Financial Partners is all about, which is asset preservation and wealth distribution.

Once people are seated, at the first appointment, we get down to the nitty gritty questions: What brought you to the workshop? What dollar amount do you need for essential income (food, clothing, shelter)? And then we get to the more fun topics, "What would you like for play money? i.e. travel, golfing, helping grandkids)." From there, our analyst team starts building income from the ground up, with foundation income (guaranteed mailbox money, come hell or high water, such as Social Security and/or pension). The difference between the amount that a client needs/wants and what they have coming that's guaranteed is what we call an "income gap." For example, if you have a retirement budget of $5000/month and Social Security/Pension income of $4000/ month, your income gap is $1000/month.

If you discover a gap, there are some tough questions to consider. Maybe you need to reduce expenses, or increase income–or a combination of both? Some folks hit this crossroads and realize that the gap is still too great, so they stay in the workforce longer than they originally planned. Pensions are slowly disappearing from American life, but for those still fortunate enough to have a pension plan at work, it's possible to retire and seek employment elsewhere, allowing them to receive a salary and pension benefit at the same time. While most folks don't have conventional pensions, there are still many union and state employees and nurses with lump sum pensions. Lump sum pensions and 401(k)s are best because we can utilize fixed indexed annuities to create self-directed pensions. After we identify income gaps, we utilize the FIA's to fill that gap.

When clients decide to work with us, we go on a deep "Fact Finder" mission to determine the mathematical particulars of their retirement. The lengthy form we have them fill out covers their secure income sources in retirement, their retirement savings, anticipated foundation expenses and anticipated discretionary expenses in retirement (all adjusted to inflation over time)–in addition to estimated effective income tax rate.

I'm pleased to say that after years of giving these seminars, most folks are usually open to hearing about these issues from me because I tend to connect well with them, and they can see that I'm sincere and dedicated to providing people with a secure retirement. But, if, for some reason, they're not "feeling" what I'm talking about or feel imposed upon when I ask them personal questions, I simply refer them elsewhere. At this point in my career, I'm secure enough to say that if I don't like someone, I simply don't do business with him or her. Working with a client is an intimate, mutual, experience driven by openness and trust, and neither side should want to try to jam a square peg into a round hole. The stakes at this stage of their lives are too high.

CHAPTER 4

HOW MUCH DO I NEED, AND FOR HOW LONG?

I'm aware that the lengthy and detailed Fact Finder form I have new clients fill out demands that they share some of the most personal information about themselves, their assets and their financial history. It's human nature for people who feel secure in what they've achieved financially to feel liberated to lay their innermost truths on the line, and for those who don't have as much as they wish they had, or have spent potential retirement money on things they now consider wasteful and foolish, to be a little more guarded about the process.

In either case, I make sure they know that I'm the least judgmental person on the planet, and that there's no shame in having made some financial mistakes in the past. They're ever-present reminders that can teach us and get us on the road to redemption. Some clients do all the right things and come to me feeling very secure emotionally and financially. Others know they've messed up and have a lot less than they had hoped. But I'm there to help them with what happens next. I tell them that no matter their history don't be afraid to share everything with me on the Fact Finder–because it's the blueprint that helps us make new history together.

In some of the client meetings I've shared in previous chapters, I talk about clients being a little nervous and skeptical, and some of the awkward moments I've had to help them through. However, once a client has decided that I'm their retirement guy and that they will trust me with their financial future, the meetings generally go smoother and we can chat like new friends intent on building exciting new memories. By that time, they've gotten to know and like what I have to say, they know I'm a no nonsense businessperson and know that I have their best interests at heart. They've filled out the Fact Finder to the best of their ability and allowed me a peek into their past and, more importantly, their needs and goals for the future.

I started the meeting with Mr. and Mrs. Melesky thinking I would take the information they gave me and ask them pretty quickly about things like "risk tolerance"–a term that essentially means, "How comfortable are you losing money?" After laughing at my joke about the length of the form ("I really don't need to know much at all, do I?"), Mrs. Melesky said, "You really should have a whole category about how much we want to visit and spoil our grandchildren."

I laughed, and she scrolled through some pictures on her cell phone and held it up. "This is Abigail and Alexis, our little cuties. They're our son's kids. They live across the country in Oregon. Abigail is starting high school in the fall and Alexis is in fifth grade and she's the star of her school's basketball team. Abigail is more into theatre. She's a great little actress and singer. We really miss them! Here, let me show you...." She flipped through photos of each of the girls, one performing in costume onstage and the other about to take a shot on the basketball court.

I looked over at Mr. Melesky, who was definitely a proud grandpa. "Wow, very impressive," I said. "Beautiful kids, very passionate about what they're doing. I can tell you're very proud of them. I don't blame you for wanting to spend as much time as possible with them." This was my opportunity to pivot into the business we came to discuss. "I'm going to help you create a plan that allows you to meet your expenses and achieve a dream retirement that allows you the money and time you need to travel, maybe even fly the girls out here to see you."

I had scheduled this meeting about a week after I started working on a plan to help them meet their monthly essentials and achieve the retirement goals they had stated on the form. But the form's facts and figures, while the foundation of all the plans we create here, can't always detect the nuances of what my clients truly desire. They may put a certain amount in the travel needs category, but when I see the kind of sparkle I saw in Mrs. Melesky's eyes when she was talking about her grandkids, that's an emotional indicator that they really want more for these trips than they wrote down. People tend to be conservative on the form, and then in conversation, as personality and emotions take over, they show that they have even more desire and ambition to achieve certain things than they have indicated. So I'm always intuiting how to make steady adjustments to any initial plan I've come up with before clients come for the meeting.

With the Meleskys, after making sure that their monthly basics were taken care of, I worked with them on finding ways to add a bit more to the amount they would have to travel. They wouldn't be spending time on Caribbean cruises or sightseeing tours of Europe, and their entertainment expenses while at home weren't extravagant, so these expenses would be very manageable.

The key to creating successful retirement plans and the perfect rate of distribution is really getting to know their priorities. I strive to always create a friendly environment where clients like The Meleskys feel comfortable about sharing their true desires rather than just what they think looks right on the Fact Finder form. The personal touch really makes a huge difference, and in the case of that wonderful couple, the plan I was able to create for them allowed them several trips a year to visit Abigal and Alexis, including a month every summer. Mrs. Melesky would often email me photos of these trips, and it was clear that the grandparents and grandchildren had a ball together. They also got to see the girls once each year during the school year, arranging things so that they could either watch one of Alexis' basketball games or Abigail's plays. Nothing gives me a greater sense of pride than making this kind of difference in my clients' lives!

TWO MAIN QUESTIONS FOR RETIREMENT

When I'm entrusted with coming up with a successful retirement plan a number of factors come into play. Like I said, the Fact Finder doesn't tell the complete picture, but it's a great objective foundation for figuring out a client's essential needs and wants. Needs include food, clothing, shelter (rent/mortgage), medical expenses and transportation.

You might be surprised at the ways small expenses add up. The items you had no trouble paying every month when funds from a salary or business were flowing in can become larger issues when you're on a fixed income stream. There are HOA Fees, utilities, TV and Internet, home phone, cell phone, home maintenance, yard/pool service, etc.

Other questions some folks need to answer is, "Are insurance and taxes included in the mortgage payment?" and "When will the mortgage be paid off?" Then we take into account monthly grocery tabs, non-Rx drugstore and clothing, and all the different types of monthly non-medical insurance payments (life, long-term care, umbrella policy, critical illness, etc.) and medical insurance payments (health, dental, Medicare premium and supplement and Rx, and what must be paid out of pocket). Transportation expenses include current auto loans, gas, insurance, maintenance and annual registration fees.

People usually have more fun filling out the "wants" page because as they estimate their monthly entertainment costs (restaurants, hobbies, movies, sports, club dues, etc.) and travel expenses (airfare, car rentals, gas, dining and shopping, activities/excursions), they're imagining having fun doing all those things.

They may just be writing numbers in boxes on a form, but those numbers translate to exciting flights of the imagination. The mind is where the concept of an ideal retirement takes shape, and then I'm there to help do the brass tacks work to turn that into reality.

In my story above about The Meleskys, I refer to risk tolerance, which is something I am obligated to ask every client about. It's as simple as, "How comfortable are you with losing money?" The options are: High? Medium? Low? At this point, most folks would say "medium to low" but that's wrong. The real answer, when it comes to retirement income money, is "NO." They can't take any risks with the money they need to live. Once we have the big picture of their needs and desires, we then put together an income plan with their income goal in mind.

We start by walking them through our process to ensure that they maximize their Social Security income and get as much from the system as possible. Many people don't realize that there are techniques available to help them get more from the government than what they see on their statements. We ask basic things like "What is your work history/wage earnings?" and "When do you want to retire?" I know it sounds like an odd question, but we also ask "How long do you expect to live?" With medical and technological breakthroughs in recent decades, the average life expectancy is longer than at any other time in history–and certainly different than it was in the 1930s when Social Security became part of America's safety net for retirees. I'm not a doctor, and I don't know everyone's genetics, but the more information I can gather about their health and family history, the better I can estimate how many years their money needs to last in retirement.

Other questions require slightly less speculation. If I'm working with a retired/retiring couple, I ask them if it's their first or second marriage. Do they have any pensions? Rental properties? Inheritances? 401(k)s, IRAs, other qualified plans, brokerage accounts, CDs, savings and other non-qualified accounts? Do they still have any dependent children? Any disabled kids that we want to ensure that they don't inherit money and lose benefits? So you see that "fact finding" is a wildly detailed process. That's why I believe trust is the foundation of everything, because I'm really asking clients to share a lot about their life up until now and what they want it to be going forward.

The Fact Finder is designed to help clients really think about their exact expenses and how much monthly income they will need during their retirement. However, filling it out is not always an easy process for people for a variety of reasons. Most folks seriously have no idea what they will need, and many assume that when their mortgage is paid off, their "Main Residence" expenses will go away, but they forget things like homeowner's insurance and taxes. People also very rarely think about "rainy day money" for unexpected events that come up like money for car repairs, house repairs or upgrades (furnace, roof, appliances, painting) and medical issues (co-pays). Maybe it's because human beings in general don't like to think about such possibilities, but most clients rarely think about setting aside a specific dollar amount for any nursing home needs that might arise as well. If they start working with me in their late 50s or early 60s, they're usually healthy and in great shape, excited to have a fun time in their retirement. It's hard to think about medical problems and declines in health during that time. Because I'm there to help them understand all the details of their retirement, it's my responsibility to tell them the importance of these issues, as unpleasant as they might be to think about. There are a lot of things that sneak up on you!

Everything related to economic issues evolves over time and so we have to plan for the reality that over the course of retirement, two major factors to consider are the rising cost of healthcare and cost of living increases. It's crucial to plan for inflation. We always factor in approximately 3-3.5% because I can promise clients that a dollar today won't buy the same goods and services in 10 and 20 years. I approach this issue in ways that are easily relatable, asking them what a movie ticket, soda or candy bar cost when they were kids. Or how much it cost per gallon to fill up their cars when they were teenagers.

I also have to lay it on the line about "wild card" issues like potential cuts to Social Security in the future of Medicare that could drive up costs. Other related issues I need to address with them include: stock market loss, change in RMD (Required Minimum Distribution) calculations, changing tax laws, changing health care laws and costs, age for Medicare, ages for Social Security eligibility, cost of living adjustments on Social Security not keeping up with inflation, pensions going under, a "look back" window on nursing home protection on assets and general inflation. Being an effective retirement planner requires very granular thinking. There are just so many fluctuating factors that people don't think about, but I make it my job to know about them so I can educate people.

In retirement planning, the second big question (after "How much income am I going to need?") is "How long do I need my money to last?" Essentially, you need it to last as long as you do. We can factor in your family history, your age, your health and how well you take care of yourself. I also inform my clients that, under the current average life expectancy statistics, an average, healthy 65 year old has a 57% chance of living until his/her 90s and an 11.5% chance of living until 100. Everyone loves those stats on the surface. I mean, who doesn't want as much time as possible on the planet and many years to enjoy retirement the way they want to enjoy it? Previous generations couldn't have fathomed having the potential to live so long on average, so we're very blessed, right? Well, yes, but only if you have money coming in at that advanced age. The only thing worse than being broke now is being broke at that age. More and more people need some form of professionally rendered care, whether it's at a facility or at home. That type of care will only increase as people continue to live longer.

Sometimes I have clients who ask, "You can do all these things, but what if I live five or ten years longer than I might plan for, and I run out of money? What happens then?" I confirm to them that it's a great question and it's smart that they are preparing for all eventualities. I then tell them to take when they expect to die and add 10 years to that age in doing the financials for their retirement. We also go one step further and plan so ultra conservatively that a client should have 30% plus left over in the end that we have factored in. One thing I have found in all the years I have been doing this is that nobody calls and complains when they have too much money.

ESSENTIAL AND DISCRETIONARY INCOME

To simplify things with new clients, I explain that I have developed a way to analyze their income needs in two main categories, Essential Income and Discretionary Income. The essential income is a main concern because it's essential that you have such things as food, clothing and shelter to survive. You can't live without it. And I believe it is important that people have discretionary income because you need some "play money" to enjoy retirement in order to thrive. I'm very much aware that the folks I work with have sacrificed most of their lives to get to this point. They shouldn't have to sacrifice in their retirement.

I distill the basic necessities of life down to three basic factors: healthcare, living expenses and taxes. There are numerous differences in how retirees living off their distribution income should view these versus the way younger working people still in the accumulation phase of their life should. During your working years, if there is a major correction or crash in the stock market, you can take a deep breath, hang on and endure a time of uncertainty because eventually the money will come back; time is on your side. Also during that time there may be inflation, but more often than not, your income will keep up with it and you have health insurance and less adverse health issues.

On the other hand, during your retirement years, you don't have the time or financial luxury of riding out a storm or crash in the market because you need that money to live on; i.e. time is NOT on your side. When it comes to inflation, Social Security doesn't always keep up with cost of living adjustments (which guys like me refer to by its acronym COLA), and Medicare supplements are necessary to help with health care. Nursing home care is also a huge concern. Every phase of life has its own share of concerns, and I always make sure my clients know about these harsher potential realities associated with the time of life we are addressing.

I like to call Discretionary Income "the wants of life" because it's "fun money," money clients want to spend for their enjoyment as they get older. Some in my industry call the whole distribution phase "playchecks for life." That's a nice turn of phrase and it captures the idea that people desire this "play money" so they can live out the joyful retirement they have been working their whole lives for. But they can only have this once their essential needs are met.

One of the reasons I love my job is that I get to help shape clients' visions of what they want their retirement years to look like. We all have hopes and dreams at different stages of our lives, and when I first began focusing my career in the financial services industry on retirement, I assumed that most retirees and pre-retirees would come to me with grand, beautiful visions of exactly how they imagined they would spend those golden years ahead. I was quickly educated otherwise. Most do not have great visions for one simple reason: they live in fear of not being ok.

I feel like our society somehow conditions us to worry about the worst things that can happen, rather than waking up excited about the best things happening. Too often we come from a mindset of deficit or lack. People are so concerned about not having enough to eat, not having enough to pay their rent or mortgage or meeting their basic expenses that they can't envision themselves looking beyond that and thinking they have the potential to achieve all their hopes and dreams.

I'm not a psychologist or sociologist, so I can't really explain why it's human nature to work from this "glass half empty" attitude, but I can create something awesome off that reality–and that is, I get the privilege of walking clients through the process and helping them see that they can have extra money and can actually think outside the box and start dreaming bigger, no matter how old they are. It's a wonderful thing to encourage them to have epiphanies about what is possible during these years, especially when they come in with a lifetime of fear based thinking driving the ship.

Generally when I talk about how people want to spend their discretionary income in retirement, I am talking about vacations, spoiling the grandkids, golf club memberships and even continuing education classes. I realize that not everyone fits into a neat little box, doing what everyone else seems to want. I tell clients, the great news is, it's YOUR retirement. You're the author of the next chapter (I guess that makes me co-writer, or at least editor!). Everyone is entitled to create their future their own unique way.

For instance, my parents like to garden and do low key things like walk on the beach and go out for coffee and socialize. Many people want to travel a little, take their grandkids to lunch on occasion or mini-golf. Others like to keep fit by going to the gym, hiking and doing yoga. And some of the more adventurous retirees even do martial arts. I have had clients want some strange things, too. One even bought a pig. I assume he had a pen in his yard!

Our 60's aren't what they were one or two generations ago. Everyone's much younger in body and spirit, and as a result, they are too healthy and too full of life to just chill out and relax all day. So many clients call this period "rehirement" instead of retirement. Because the 60's are no longer old, people can still work (supplementing the income I help them achieve) and do volunteer work with charities and political organizations in their community.

The main thing to remember when we're talking about Essential and Discretionary income is that Essential comes before Discretionary. Food and shelter is more important than golf or buying and feeding pigs! But even if folks live on a tight budget they can enjoy a lifestyle like my parents, a little simpler and less extravagant but no less enjoyable and exciting. I'm kind of like them, appreciating the simple pleasures. I love the ocean, ponds and spending time in my backyard. You can live a full life if you focus, like I do, on spirituality and nature. Meditation and being near the water works wonders for the human soul.

CREATING THE PLAN

So let's review the process of creating plans for our clients. First we meet and gather the info about their work history, assets, rental properties, pension, when they want to retire and how long they expect to live. Then the analysts we work with put together a report, we review it with the clients and discuss which strategy works best. We identify any income gaps, then implement the plan to close those with guaranteed protected income for life, then review consistently and revise as necessary over the coming months and years.

For this to work effectively, we must get to know the client's personal life situation, goals and concerns. Then we put together a plan to meet these goals or at least the majority of them and we accomplish closing the income gap with guaranteed predictable income for life. Once we've tailored those needs to the client's current economic situation and personality, our main focus shifts to creating this reliable income. There are several ways to make it happen.

We first utilize strategies to maximize Social Security, then assess any other income sources a client may have, such as a rental property and pension. From there, we analyze the difference between what their goals are and what they have coming in, and fill the gap using 401(k)s, IRAs and other retirement savings.

Like I stated earlier regarding the fear factor, people are often afraid that they don't or won't have enough or it isn't in the right place or they don't know where to pull from. They were raised by parents who grew up in The Great Depression so they have this fear built in. I think I am effective at what I do because while it seems that the majority of Americans run their lives based on fear, for whatever reason–maybe because I'm just so happy to be alive and healthy after struggling with addiction for so many years–I am an optimist and realist. I bring positivity to every meeting and it's usually very infectious.

My hope is that the clients will not only feel and share my upbeat, optimistic energy but understand the reasons behind it. Once I put a solid, concrete plan together and they understand the details of it and how they will benefit from it, they know where I'm coming from and leave with a sense of hope and confidence about their future. That's the ultimate high for me now.

CHAPTER 5

WHAT ANNUITIES CAN DO

By the time I get around to talking about annuities with my clients, we've already established a strong sense of mutual trust, an easygoing, free-flowing business friendship, and a feeling that everything we say to each other will be truthful and direct. I consider annuities my "bread and butter," the expertise I am most proud of and most excited to discuss because using them properly and effectively is the surest way to distribute a lifetime of guaranteed income that keeps my clients sleeping soundly at night.

My favorite kind of annuities meeting is one in which the clients come into the conference room bursting with things to tell me about the research they've done. Like I said earlier, I am aware that part of my job is to educate retirees about all the details related to how we can secure their retirement income for years to come—but it's always helpful when they are already armed with some of the basic terminology and general concepts we are going to talk about.

The first few times we met, Mr. and Mrs. Sumrall both began the small talk with anecdotes about their favorite Red Sox and Celtics players of all time, and their desire to have enough extra income in retirement to buy season tickets for both of their beloved hometown teams every year for the rest of their lives, assuming they had good health and mobility. But I had hinted that this meeting would be the one where we would discuss the brass tacks of investment products. I briefly mentioned the word "annuity" and that got them Googling up a storm.

Even before he sat down, Mr. Sumrall said, "Ryan, did you know that annuities have actually been around for hundreds of years. They were known as 'annua' in the days of the Roman Empire. In 225 AD, a judge in Rome named Ulpianus produced the first mortality table."

"Hey, I thought I was supposed to be the expert," I laughed. "Tell me more."

Clearly, Mrs. Sumrall was up to speed on the history of annuities as well. She chimed in, "They also called that the 'actuarial life table.' The modern annuities you guys use today have only existed a few decades, but the idea of paying out a stream of income dates back to those times. The Latin word meant annual stipends and during the reign of the emperors it meant a contract that made annual payments. Roman soldiers were paid annuities as a form of compensation for military service."

"And during the Middle Ages, they were used by feudal lords and kings to help cover the heavy costs of their wars and conflicts."

I couldn't resist: "I'm glad you'll be using yours for more fun things like vacations and visiting the grandkids. If the kids start fighting you can remind them of this, though."

"One more thing," Mr. Sumrall said. "We read that annuities first came to America in 1759 in the form of a retirement pool for church pastors in Pennsylvania. They provided a lifetime stream of income for ministers and their families. Ben Franklin left the cities of Philly and Boston each an annuity in his will. And here's the kicker, the Boston annuity paid out until the early 1990s because the city decided to stop receiving payments and take a lump-sum distribution of the remaining balance."

"That's great news," I laughed. "So we'll be in good shape if you guys live to be over 200! You know, with modern medicine these days, you never know..."

"We'll take 30, God-willing," Mrs. Sumrall said.

The meeting was off to what I call a warm, friendly start, with them beaming with pride at what they already knew (which to be honest was more than I did about the history) and ready to talk about the way modern Fixed Indexed Annuities were going to help them. Not every client comes in with those kinds of cool anecdotes about annuities, but every one of them is eager to know how we work with them to fund their retirement.

THE ESSENTIALS OF ANNUITIES

So here are the basics, as I explain it to my clients: Annuities are investment vehicles offered by insurance companies. They offer tax advantages in some situations, in addition to principal protection, earning interest in different ways, and guaranteed income for life.

There are many different types. We focus on Fixed Indexed Annuities because they offer the client protection of their principal, ability to earn good interest when the market goes up and then locks in the gains so that those are protected from market loss and fluctuation. The income can be guaranteed for a specific period of time, or for the rest of a client's life. Fixed annuities may also be structured to pay over joint or multiple lives. They can pay income now, which are known as Immediate Income Annuities, or later, which are better known as Deferred Income Annuities. Immediate annuities are set up to pay an income for a set number of years (five, ten, fifteen, twenty). The client would make a deposit, and the life insurance company will pay a fixed rate over that period. The catch is, once the allotted time of payments is over, the income stops and the funds are gone. For obvious reasons, most of the annuities owned by people today are in the deferred category.

At the time the contract is opened, the client chooses the term, which is the number of years until the principal is guaranteed and the surrender period is finished. In a bull market, they will not achieve the actual performance of the index due to the formulas, spreads, participation rates and caps applied to Fixed Indexed Annuities, as well as because of the absence of dividends. But in a down (bear) market, the client won't ever lose their principal, assuming that the underlying insurance company stays solvent.

Fixed Indexed Annuities offer certain features that most investments don't, such as nursing home riders, which help pay for the cost of nursing home care, enhanced death benefit, protection of principle (whereby a client's money is insured) and income riders which ensure that the clients receive income for life. This is the tool we use to build self-directed pensions as well. A few basic definitions are in order here. An income rider is an attached benefit to a deferred annuity policy that solves for longevity risk by providing a lifetime income stream. They typically have a guaranteed growth rate that can be used for income, and can be flexible from a planning standpoint. A self-directed pension may be suitable for experienced investors who want to manage their pension fund investments themselves. It allows access to invest in a range of fixed-interest and equity securities.

There are certain questions all my clients ask me when the annuities discussion begins, and the Sumralls were no exception. They may have known their history, but they were also thinking about their future security.

So they, like many of my clients, asked, "Is my money safe?" (You know it!)

"What are the fees?" (They vary, but roughly half that of a mutual fund in a 401(k).)

"Why don't more people use this?" (It's not as highly marketed as it should be.)

"Will this protect me from the next 2008-esque crash like crazy?" (It's bulletproof. We lock in the peaks and avoid the pits.)

"How long until I can get my money?" (Clients can start to take income within the first year.)

"Does my family get the money when I die?" (Every penny!)

When it comes to detailing the benefits of Fixed Indexed Annuities, and how they fit into a client's monthly financial needs, I break things down very simply. I use the tools I have to measure and fill the income gap first. For example, if a client needs $5,000 to live on each month, receives $3,000 from Social Security and has a $2,000 shortfall, I put enough money into a FIA for that client to ensure that they will ALWAYS meet their income goals regardless of what the market does. After all, you can't tell the gas, electric or cable company, "I can't pay...the market's down this week!"

I remember one couple came to me with a nest egg of $800,000 and wanted $5,000 a month to live on. Social Security provided $3,000 so they were short $2,000. We put $500,000 into an FIA which guaranteed the clients $25,000 per year to fill that gap. It boils down to simple math.

One of the most important questions they ask is, "How do you create a secure income stream?" I explain that we use the FIA to ensure that the income is guaranteed monthly. We move either their retirement money (401(k), IRA, etc.) or non-qualified money such as brokerage accounts, CD's or savings into an FIA and use that to provide income that's guaranteed while still allowing the principal to grow.

CLEARING UP MISCONCEPTIONS

Although annuities can offer great value to their holders, there are many misconceptions about how they work and who they will benefit–and believe me, I've heard them all when discerning clients come in with skeptical articles and objections. In 2013, I read an article on the Senior Financial Advisors Bridge website about the Ten Biggest Misconceptions about Annuities. The top ones were 1) Fixed annuities come with huge surrender penalties; 2) All annuities charge high fees; 3) Annuities are difficult to understand; and 4) The money put into an annuity is all tied up; and 5) Nothing is left for my family when I die.

Let's knock those down one by one. The insurance company charges a surrender penalty only if the annuity is redeemed ahead of schedule. If we're talking about variable annuities, they sometimes come with high fees because multiple parties are involved in their manufacture and distribution. But variable annuities and fixed indexed annuities are very different. As for being complicated, when you come down to the basics, fixed annuities are fairly simple. You give your money to an insurance company, and in return they pay you interest, via a contract for a certain period of time. As for the "tied up" objection, there are always some strings attached to getting 100% of your money back. Annuities are flexible and provide many options, and you always know what you're getting into. Now, the last one about nothing being left for your family when you die… with a pension, income lasts for the employee's life and sometimes, the spouse's life. Upon their deaths, nothing goes to their children. That's how they are structured, for maximum income for their lives. You can do the same with most annuities–and only an annuity– not a stock, bond, mutual fund or other non-annuity investment. Only annuities offer the option of converting your money to a guaranteed lifetime income you cannot outlive.

One of the biggest problems fueling these misconceptions is that years ago, advisors used SPIA's, or Single Premium Immediate Annuities, where you give the insurance company money and they pay you till you die. So if you die early, they keep the money and win. But if you're like my grandfather, "Stan the Man," who is in his 90's, then you win because you got more from the system.

It seems grossly inequitable, and most advisors with common sense don't use these, but sadly (to me anyway), they're still often used in pensions.

The other big problem is one I alluded to above—variable annuities. These have a wide range of investment options. Most common are fund portfolios that offer a rate of return on the performance of the options you choose. The difference is, they are securities, and the periodic payments you ultimately receive will vary greatly due to the fluctuation of the mutual fund. These are so far different from the guaranteed annuities I use for my retiree clients, and I believe they're best suited for younger investors who can withstand such market risks.

While I'm not a fan in general of variable annuities, some of them offer an income rider (which grows at a guaranteed rate for a future income stream), but the cash value could go to zero on these and my clients need an enduring cash value in case they need a roof, furnace, or some other extraordinary repair or maintenance, or simply want to take a vacation. Variable annuities are heavy on fees. Both of these annuities I have mentioned have been the other annuities' black eye, and it's easy for those uneducated about annuities to be confused or assume things that aren't true. But that's where I come in, to shed light on the differences and let clients know I would only use products that would guarantee them income for life. The Fixed Indexed Annuity is the best tool for the income portion of my clients' portfolios.

I think the bad rap given to the term "annuities" happens the way it does in any other industry. A few bad companies cause problems for the rest of us. For example, some have higher fees, no protection of principal, caps (which means limits on what a client can earn) and spreads that can change. That being said, however, all of my well versed, educated and savvy clients ask for these to provide guaranteed income for life. These work the same as a self-directed pension. Ask anyone if they would like a pension and they'll say yes, because these are like pensions where you actually own the nest egg. Best of both worlds!

I tell all my clients that FIAs provide solid returns over the long term. What I mean by this is, mutual funds, stocks and bonds go up but unless you sell at the right time, they creak when the market does like we learned in 2008–so those are just paper gains, meaning they look good on paper but aren't tangible assets you can work with. Annuities lock in your gains, which make them solid gains because they're real, and no market downturn can take them away. The true measuring stick is how an investment does in a down market. By locking in the peaks and avoiding the pits, we ensure that the annuity pays higher retirement income because it's paying out from a larger bucket of money that NEVER experiences losses.

So let's summarize the differences. Fixed Income Annuities have lower fees, the principal is fully insured, all gains are locked in and insured and they have guaranteed income riders that, like a self-funded pension, provide income for life. You can't lose anything but there is an upside tied to positive market performance. Variable Annuities, on the other hand, have very high fees, and there is the potential that a client can lose all the cash value of the initial investment. VA can offer income riders, but at a very high cost. These are not suitable for my clients.

ENGAGING IN THE PROCESS

Because every client's needs are different, there's no single financial scenario I can use, numbers wise, to illustrate how I work to find him or her the perfect annuity products to ensure future financial security. However, I can say this, everything is grounded in a similar process. We get to know them, their background, their hopes and dreams, their essential needs and their ideal vision for the future, and work the numbers and products from that information and personal connection. If I want to get in shape, I spend time at the gym. If I want peace and serenity in my life, I spend time meditating and praying. If I want to service my clients, I need to spend time getting to know them…their goals, their fears and their financials. Then and only then can I work with my team to find the right tools and products.

I would say that my clients The Sumralls went above and beyond in discovering all that historical information about annuities. While most clients don't go that far, I'm happy to report that these days, most people I work with know someone who has an annuity and they hear positive things about the safety they provide, so they come in already having dispensed with those objections I mentioned. If they're pro-annuity coming into the meeting, all the better, but they're still usually curious about just how they work and, more importantly, how they can work to their benefit. But it's not one size fits all so I let them know from the start that we have work to do.

The majority of them know that the money is 100% safe, and that it's tax deferred with non-qualified money. But few know in advance about the income rider element, the different strategies we can use to accumulate interest, or the strong ability they have to earn and keep interest. I have a number of ways in which I educate them, and I have to admit that sometimes this is my favorite part. There's nothing like seeing the light go on in people's eyes when they finally understand something they came in confused about.

I mentioned earlier in the book about the workshops I do in Social Security planning and building a retirement income. I also have a radio show, send out monthly educational emails and a website full of great information. My goal with Summit Financial is to really service our clients in a multitude of ways—some might say "over the top," but that's the only way I know how to do things, full throttle! All the great leaders in history, from Jesus and Gandhi to Abraham Lincoln and Martin Luther King, Jr. had what the Bible calls a "servant's heart." Leaders serve others. I choose to serve, too.

MY DISCOVERY OF ANNUITIES

I humbly admit that earlier in my career, I was very much focused on funds, stocks and so on. But there came a point–I think it was back in 2003–when I started hating having to explain to family and friends how the market was down and we "just had to ride out the storm" and "It always comes back." I was a jumble of clichés trying to justify my investments and to encourage others. "You win some, you lose some," "Six and one half a dozen the other," "Taking one step back to take two forward..." I tried to convince myself there was truth to these expressions, but ultimately I realized they were all just sales talk, all nonsense, and totally unacceptable.

In 2004, a very wealthy man sat with me and he asked specifically for this tool I only had a passing understanding of, annuities. I did some research and I fell in love. Once it hit me that an advisor could give clients all this upside potential without ever having to apologize for the market being down, I was hooked. I wanted the chance to give my clients guaranteed income for life–LIFE–and so annuities became the focal point of my work with retirees.

The first person I used annuities with was the intelligent man who requested that approach, but the first person I selected it for and presented it to after that was in a way kind of magical. As I write this, I'm 26,000 miles in the air flying to see Wayne in Florida. Wayne became a client in the early 2000s. In 2005, we used annuities as the tool to protect his hard earned nest egg from the gas company. It's no coincidence that it was him and his very special wife, Jackie. God doesn't do coincidences. It was definitely what I like to call a "God shot." We love Wayne and Jackie. It was awesome and felt like a dream. They've been with me for 17 years now, and they are far more than just "clients" to me. They stuck with me through my tough times. Wayne said, "I don't give up on good people and you're a good person."

I think the greatest proof that annuities work to keep my clients' money safe is what happened for this great couple after the crash in 2008. While everyone else who had different kinds of market investments lost 38% or more of their funds, Wayne's cash value didn't lose a penny and his income account actually increased 7%!

I'm very proud of these success stories, but I prefer not to use those kinds of anecdotes to try to overcome any skepticism that a client may bring to the discussion about annuities. I simply let the clients express their concerns and goals. While they're doing that, they usually end up describing something that sounds very much like a FIA! In the few cases they don't, we give them other options. The bottom line is, I want them to be happy because it's their hard earned nest egg that we're working with. As their advisor, it's my job to offer suggestions, but they need to make protecting it a priority.

ARE ANNUITIES ALWAYS THE RIGHT CHOICE?

By now, it should be clear that I am a huge fan of Fixed Indexed Annuities and I have spent years using them to help people secure their retirement, and talking them up any chance I get. So, when people ask me whether they are always the right choice, I share my passion in a slightly humbler and more objective way. It's never all or nothing, but for money that's needed to provide income for those current and future needs and wants we've been talking about, over the first 10-15 years of retirement, I think it's a solid choice. It's the best solution I have found for the simple reason that it provides that ROI (Reliability of Income) we talked about in Chapter Three. It's guaranteed monthly income, come hell or high water!

That said, there are a few people for whom I would say that a FIA might not be appropriate—mainly, folks with huge pensions and lots of rental properties that enjoy riding the tide of the ups and downs in the market, playing it as a challenge or a sport, with unlimited funds to draw from. We call these clients "cowboys" because they love the rush and enjoy living in the unpredictability of what is truly a modern equivalent of the Wild, Wild West.

I'm always game to share the kinds of clients annuities aren't right for, but if you start asking me about the typical client whom they are the perfect thing for, I'll have a lot more to say because that's the majority of them who seek my expertise. Essentially, FIA are right for folks that have a discrepancy between what they want for income and what their Social Security payments provide. It's right for those who don't want to feel the pain they felt in 2008, when the institutions we thought we could trust let us down and took so much of our investments with them. It's exactly right for those who want the opportunity to enjoy their day to day life, their grandkids and travel (both to visit family, and for vacations) no matter what happens on Wall Street that day or week.

FIA are also for people who are tired of paying high fund and advisor fees. Because even in years like 2008 when the market lost 38% of its value, clients paid 3% in fees on top of that just to be in the game. Yes, that's right–they PAID TO LOSE MONEY! Does that make any sense at all? I wouldn't pay my mechanic to break my car. I think that's the perfect metaphor for exactly what you don't want to happen with your nest egg, and why Fixed Income Annuities are the best way to prevent that.

Again, in all fairness, I have to add that the only real pitfall with a FIA is their lack of liquidity. Most of the good ones allow a client to withdraw 10% plus growth (which should far exceed what a sensible client takes out), but for clients that want more freedom, we can build them out with more liquidity to meet their needs and desires.

The role of Fixed Income Annuities is to provide guaranteed, predictable and sustainable income for life that keeps up with inflation. It's the only tool of its kind that allows me to shake a client's hand and say, "I guarantee this money will be in your account regardless of what Wall Street storms we encounter."

A decade after the crash that led to the Great Recession, the confidence I bring to that statement is great news for retirees everywhere who want nothing more than to sleep soundly at night while waking up every day happy and excited about enjoying the rest of their lives.

CHAPTER 6

MAXIMIZING WHAT YOU ALREADY HAVE

One of my favorite parts of retirement planning is watching the happily surprised looks on clients' faces when I tell them they have–or can legally work the system to obtain–more money than they thought they had or were entitled to. I use the phrase "maximizing what you already have" to illustrate for them how we can use the right financial tools and strategies to get the most out of their retirement savings that they have right now. Their eyes sometimes literally light up when it hits them that I'm able to eliminate their need to count on or hope for a rate of growth that may no longer be achievable due to their age or the shrinking years they have left to earn money via regular employment.

This is true for those that are already retired, of course, but it also applies to those who expect to retire within 10 years or so. The clients who are most grateful to hear this are the "average" retirees who have saved a nice nest egg for retirement but are not rich. With planning that is focused on maximizing what they already have, more often than not, they can achieve a comfortable and sustainable retirement lifestyle.

When I do my seminars on topics like Social Security, the folks who attend often ask, "What's the most important thing in retirement?" My response is my mantra: "Cash flow is king!" That's because it's how they pay their bills and pay for their fun.

It's interesting that in financial planning circles, a lot of attention is paid to clients' "net worth," but having a certain amount on paper doesn't mean they can pay their monthly bills. I'll tell them, "Let's say you own $1 million worth of land, and that land does not produce income. You may be a millionaire on paper, but you can't pay your bills, or have play money, unless you sell the land." So where does the cash flow come from? By maximizing the income that can be generated from the savings and investments they already have. It's not just a matter of getting the most return on their money to use as income, it's about ensuring that the income generated from those savings is reliable and sustainable over their lifetime.

Some folks are lucky in that their investments include rental properties that produce income, and a small (and unfortunately dwindling) percentage may get pensions from their employers. For most Americans though, retirement income security comes from two main sources: their qualified retirement plans such as 401(k) and their Social Security benefits.

There are a lot of different factors that go into determining those Social Security benefits, so it's crucial to understand some of the key rules that help you maximize your benefits. One of those–and one that I find a lot of clients are unaware of until I tell them the good news–is the Spousal Benefit. I'll never forget the day Mr. and Mrs. Gentry sat down nervously across from me at the conference table and told me that based on what they believed they were entitled to from Uncle Sam every month, they would fall $1,000 short of meeting their monthly expenses. They had a small nest egg that they wanted to place in annuities, but they didn't plan to live extravagantly at least the first few years of their retirement. They were determined not to turn on the income stream from these riders until further down the line when they absolutely needed it. Their success at achieving this goal depended on whether I could make their Social Security income work better for them.

"I guess we're old school, but Mary spent most of our married life as a homemaker raising our kids," Mr. Gentry said, "and when they were on their own, she decided to do volunteer work in our community and start a small jewelry making business. So I don't think she has a personal benefit...I guess we didn't think of the ramifications of this down the road."

"I definitely understand," I said. "Sometimes we get busy enjoying life on our own terms, doing what we love or are passionate about, and don't really want to worry about those things." Both of them looked downcast, as if they were ashamed of something, but before either could respond, I asked, "What do you know about the Spousal benefits?"

"Spousal what?" Mrs. Gentry perked up.

"Don't worry, a lot of clients I meet haven't heard of them, but they're amazing," I said. "They're just the ticket for situations like yours where Mary doesn't have the so called official 'lifetime earnings' to get her own benefit. Personally, I admire women who devote their lives to raising their kids, start their own home businesses and do volunteer work. I spend a lot of my time outside the office helping people. I wish the government would value these kinds of things more."

"We all do," Mr. Gentry said. "So tell us more."

"What if I told you that the Spousal Benefit can increase your total household Social Security benefits by as much as 50%?"

"Throw us some numbers, Ryan," Mrs. Gentry said.

So I told them the basics. The spouse of a Social Security recipient is eligible to receive the larger of the two benefit calculations–the monthly benefit based upon their own work record or the monthly amount based upon the spouse's work record, which is 50% of their spouse's monthly benefit at their spouse's full retirement age. I told them they met the Spousal Benefit requirement because they had been married more than a year (42, actually!), they were both over 62 and Mr. Gentry had filed for his own benefits. I also gave them the good news that because Mr. Gentry had waited until his full retirement age, their benefit would be the full 50% of his Primary Insurance Benefit.

Numbers wise, here's how it worked for the Gentrys: David's Primary Insurance Amount is $2,000 a month, which meant that Mary could claim her Spousal Benefit of $1,000 monthly. So they could increase their combined household Social Security income from $2,000 to $3,000, an increase of 50%! Needless to say they were thrilled, and told me that this extra $1,000 would help them meet the expenses they had been worrying about.

As an aside, let's say Mary had worked part time most of her life and qualified for a $500 monthly benefit on her own. The Spousal Benefit would still be $500 more than that. So by not officially "working"–that is, a regular job with taxable income– she actually gets more from Social Security than if she had. It sounds crazy, but that's one very cool part of what's usually a pretty complex system!

UNDERSTANDING AND MAXIMIZING SOCIAL SECURITY BENEFITS

Social Security Benefits are the bedrock of retirement income for the majority of Americans, providing a significant portion of total retirement income. This is true not only for those with little savings, but also for those so called "average" retirees that have accumulated some retirement savings. Let's think about this: a monthly benefit of $2000 provides $256,865 over ten years, and $554,968 in income over 20 years (assuming a 1.5% Cost of Living increase). This is a significant amount for the vast majority of Americans.

The key to maximizing your Social Security benefits begins

with deciding when to best begin your benefits. As a general rule, you typically want to wait as long as possible to begin your benefits, because the longer you wait, the larger your monthly benefit. The amount you receive each month is based on what we call a "Primary Insurance Amount" or PIA for short. Your PIA is the monthly amount you will receive when you attain Full Retirement Age. This is based upon a complex calculation related to how much you earned over your lifetime (in addition to other factors). I don't need to go into the U.S. government's math, but I recently read an article in the *USA Today* called "8 Social Security Rules You Need to Know." Rule No. 1 was "Your base benefits are determined by your 35 highest income years." That means if you worked more than that, the rest of your work history and the money you paid into Social Security does not count towards your benefits calculation.

It's important to know that everybody's Primary Insurance Amount is different. It depends on how much you earned over your lifetime that was subject to Social Security taxation, which one of the taxes within the FICA (Federal Insurance Contribution Act) you're subject to and withholding from your paychecks (or that you pay yourself if you're self-employed). Your full retirement age depends on the year you were born. If your birth year is from 1943 to 1954, then your full retirement age is 66. For those born after 1954 but before 1960, the Full Retirement Age increases in monthly increments until the birth year of 1960 (and beyond) when it is age 67.

Regardless of your Full Retirement Age, you can choose to receive benefits as early as age 62, and you can wait as long as age 70. The age at which you claim benefits determines how much of your Primary Insurance Amount you will receive. Keep in mind Rule No. 4 from the same *USA Today* article: Taking Benefits early will cost you forever. The author, Wendy Connick, writes, "Start taking benefits at age 62...and your benefits will be reduced by as much as 30% for the rest of your life." This would translate to receiving $1500 a month (if you start at 62) vs. $2000 a month (if you start at 66). If you waited until 70, you would get $2,640 per month instead of $2000 (at age 66).

The bottom line is, the first step in maximizing Social Security benefits is to wait as long as you can to start your benefits–and understanding the potential power of the Spousal Benefit where it applies. In helping you determine when to best begin receiving your benefits, there are several types of analysis that financial professionals like myself use to determine what is optimal for your situation based on your specific circumstances. You should have this done as part of your retirement planning. In addition to Social Security benefit analysis, there are other factors that also should be considered that impact when it would be most beneficial to claim your Social Security benefits.

Another important consideration in determining when to let your Social Security begin is if you have any other sources of retirement income such as pensions or income from rental properties, and the level of your retirement savings. If these other income sources, including the amount you can generate from savings, are sufficient to meet your income needs without Social Security benefits, then it often makes sense to wait until age 70 to start Social Security benefits because doing so will provide the highest monthly benefit.

Even if you think you have enough savings to cover your expenses during your 60s, and waiting might make sense on the surface, here's something important to consider. Let's assume that your benefit at age 66 is $2000 monthly, and $2,640 at age 70. If you wait until 70 to claim benefits, and you need that $2000 a month to pay your bills, this means you must take that $2000 a month out of your savings. From ages 66 to 70, that's $96,000 taken from savings.

As you can see, the decision as to when to best start your Social Security benefits is dependent on a lot of different, individualized factors that can require some complex analysis. The analysis must include not only when to best take Social Security benefits based on maximizing them, but also the application of different benefit start ages, and therefore different monthly amounts. Only by looking at this big picture over a 20 to 25 year projection can you truly maximize the impact of Social Security benefit income within your overall retirement income plan. I've found that more often than not, the thing we call our Retirement Income Forecast reveals that it's better to begin the Social Security benefits earlier rather than later because then you won't need to withdraw as much from your nest egg to make ends meet.

Ultimately, maximizing what you already have means making your entire retirement income plan provide you with the best overall balance of SS income, other income sources, and income generated from your savings to ensure that your retirement income lasts for your (and your spouse's) lifetime.

UNDERSTANDING AND MAXIMIZING PENSION OPTIONS

For much of the 20th Century, most large employers offered pensions to their employees who worked for the required number of years, but in the 21st Century United States, this has changed a lot. Specifically a pension is a "Defined Benefit Plan," meaning that the retirement income benefit from the employer is defined typically as a percentage of the employee's earnings based upon a formula. We can contrast this with the more common Defined Contribution Plan such as a 401(k), in which the contribution by the employer to the retirement plan is defined, typically as a percentage of earnings or as a percentage of what the employee saves to the retirement plan.

The pension statistics are pretty sobering. In the early 80s, about 60% of private sector employers offered pensions, whereas now only about 4% of private sector employers offer a pension; these days about 14% of these private sector employers offer a combination of both a Defined Benefit Plan and a Defined

Contribution Plan. A 2012 article I found on workforce.com illustrates the changes that have happened over the past few generations. From 1940 to 1960, the number of people covered by private pensions increased from 3.7 million to 19 million, or nearly 30 percent of the labor force, according to the Employee Benefit Research Institute. By 1975, 103,346 plans covered 40 million people. In 1983, there were 175,143 plans but by 2008, there were only 46,926 plans, and the numbers have been shrinking since. The private sector employees that still offer pensions are typically in industries with a strong union presence in their workforce, and reducing or eliminating the pension plan is an almost constant goal of private sector employers. Most government employees still have a pension plan, however, with about 84% of state and local governments providing a Defined Benefit Plan; almost all federal employees are also covered by this kind of plan.

Why have pensions been disappearing? Simple–cost and ongoing liability. Historically, it's been more costly for employers to offer pensions because it costs them more over time than Defined Contribution Plans, and those costs are somewhat unpredictable. As a simple example, if as an employer, you define the dollar amount of the retirement benefit many years down the road, your cost to keep that promise can go up significantly if the investments supporting that promised pension produce lower returns than expected. When this happens, the employer has to add more money to the pension plan, and this of course impacts their profits. With a Defined Contribution Plan, the cost to the employer is more predictable, and the employer is not responsible for ensuring that a specific dollar amount of retirement income is achieved for the employee.

So what does all this background info have to do with you? If you don't have a pension plan, it's just a sobering history lesson. However, if you do, then at retirement you'll have to make some important decisions. Most pension plans will offer you several different choices for your pension, and each choice will affect the dollar amount you receive each month, and the dollar amount your surviving spouse will receive after your death.

Your choices may look something like this:

Option A: Life Only Benefit. This will pay you the highest monthly dollar amount, but upon your death, your surviving spouse will not receive anything at all (If you are married, you can only choose this option if your spouse agrees to it in writing). This may also be called a "Life Only Annuity Payment."

Option B: 50% Survivor Benefit. This will pay you a lesser monthly dollar amount than the Life Only Benefit option while you are alive, and at your death will pay your surviving spouse 50% of your benefit for their remaining lifetime. This may also be called a "50% Survivor Annuity."

Option C: 100% Survivor Benefit. This will pay you a lesser monthly dollar amount than either the Life Only Benefit option or the 50% Survivor Benefit option, and at your death your surviving spouse will receive 100% of your benefit for their remaining lifetime. This may also be called a "100% Survivor Annuity."

Option D: Life with 10 Year Certain Benefit. This will pay you less than the Life Only Benefit option while you are alive, but possibly more than the 50% Survivor Benefit option and the 100% Survivor Benefit options. This means that if you die before collecting 10 years of benefits, the remainder of the monthly payments for the 10 years will be paid to your surviving spouse. If you die after collecting at least 10 years of benefits, your surviving spouse will not receive anything at all. This may also be called a "Life with 10 Years Certain Annuity."

Option E: Lump Sum Payout Benefit. This is a one-time distribution to you of the current dollar value of your pension. Basically, you take the money and it is up to you to create income from it. Typically a lump-sum payout is rolled-over into an IRA to avoid taxation on the lump-sum.

So how do you know the best option? As with everything involving retirement income planning, it depends upon your individual situation, including your income needs and desires, your other income sources, your Social Security benefits, your savings and, of course, whether or not you are married.

This decision must be analyzed in the "big picture" to see what makes the most sense for you. If you have a lot of savings or income sources that will continue after your death (such as rental properties), then it might be best to take the highest payout and no Survivor Benefit if it appears that you have enough savings to create income for your surviving spouse when you die. Similarly, if you have life insurance that will provide enough money to your surviving spouse to create sufficient income for your spouse at your death, then it might be best to take the highest payout and no Survivor Benefit. In general, financial professionals will recommend an option that does provide a Survivor Benefit, as the loss of pension benefits and reduced Social Security benefits at the first death of a married couple is a chief contributor to reduced standards of living or even poverty in old age, especially for women.

One technique I have found that works well for many married couples is commonly referred to as "pension maximization." This technique utilizes a life insurance policy on the Pensioners life, and therefore pays the Surviving Spouse a large sum of money at the Pensioners death. In a nutshell, this involves choosing the Life Only Benefit option to maximize the monthly pension income, and paying a life insurance premium to protect the Surviving Spouse. How well this can work depends upon the health and age of the Pensioner because this determines the cost of the life insurance. If the cost of the life insurance is less than the difference between the Life Only Benefit option pension's income and the reduced pension income from the options that provide a Spousal Benefit, then it can be very effective.

One other note about pensions: If you have the choice to take a lump-sum distribution of your pension benefit, the decision whether or not to take the lump-sum option instead of one of the lifetime income options must be weighed very carefully, but in many cases it may be a good option for you.

Perhaps the greatest factor to consider is, how "healthy" is the pension plan? Many, if not most, private corporation and state/ municipal pension plans are significantly underfunded, meaning that they are "on the hook" for more future benefits than they are projected to have the assets to pay. This problem is not limited to the plans of smaller companies. This is equally true for some of the largest corporations in the world. If a pension plan is significantly underfunded, then to meet the current and future obligations to the pensioners the plan sponsor must either add a lot more money to the plan (or get better investment results), or eventually reduce both current and promised benefits. If benefits are reduced, you could find that the pension income you counted on could be reduced in the future at precisely the time you need it (when you are already retired).

WHAT TO DO WITH YOUR RETIREMENT PLAN, IRA AND OTHER SAVINGS AT RETIREMENT

For clarity, let's first be sure we understand the difference between the tax-status of different types of accounts and the investments that are held within an account, as this is a commonly confused issue.

First, there are three broad categories of accounts by tax status. First, there are "Non-Qualified Accounts." "Non-Qualified" is not an official term, but it is commonly used to describe any type of account that is not a Qualified Retirement Plan or an IRA (described below). You save money in these types of accounts after-tax, the taxation on the growth of the account depends upon the specific type of investments within the account and in some cases how long you hold the investments, and there is no requirement to take withdrawals from the account.

Next are Qualified Retirement Plans, meaning accounts such as 401(k), 403(b), 457 plans and other "alphabet soup" titles. These are employer sponsored retirement savings plans that you (and your employer) contribute to while you are working. Your contributions to these plans are made pre-tax, the growth of the money is tax-deferred, and when you withdraw money it is fully taxable as ordinary income. You are penalized if you withdraw money prior to age 59 1/2 (there are exceptions to this), and you must begin to take withdrawals from these plans beginning at age 70 ½. Increasingly, many employer plans offer a "Roth 401(k)" choice which functions like the Roth IRA described below.

Finally, there are Individual Retirement Arrangements or "IRA." There a few versions of these, but from a tax status viewpoint they work for the most part just like Qualified Retirement Plans, except that they are individual plans instead of employer plans. Your savings contributions are pre-tax, the growth of the money is tax-deferred, and when you withdraw money it is fully taxable as ordinary income. You are penalized if you withdraw money prior to age 59 ½ (there are exceptions to this), and you must begin to take withdrawals from these plans beginning at age 70 ½ (more about that later). The exception is the "Roth IRA." With a Roth IRA, your savings are contributed after-tax, but growth is tax-free as are withdrawals, and there is generally no requirement to ever withdraw the money in the account.

For the most part, you can own any kind of investment within any of these types of accounts. Put differently (and for clarity), a 401(k) is not an "investment," it is just the tax status of the account. The mutual fund you own inside the 401(k) is the investment, and you could own that very same mutual fund inside of a "non-qualified" account.

Now a word about Required Minimum Distributions: The requirement to start withdrawing money from a 401(k) or IRA is known as "Required Minimum Distributions," or "RMD." The amount of your annual RMD is a function of two things: your age, and the balance of your account. Specifically, your age corresponds to a schedule of factors published by the IRS. There are three different schedules, but most people are required to use what is called the "Uniform Schedule" for calculating annual RMD. The Uniform Schedule assigns a "Life Expectancy Factor" for each age from 70 through age 115, with these factors getting smaller each year. The effect of these factors getting smaller each year is that every year, you are required to withdraw a larger percentage of your tax-qualified plan.

It is an easy calculation. You simply divide your account balance on December 31st of the previous year by the factor corresponding to your age; the result is the minimum dollar amount you must withdraw.

When you retire, you have the choice of keeping your savings in your Qualified Retirement Plan such as your 401(k), or you can choose to transfer your money from the 401(k) to an IRA; doing this is commonly called a "rollover." If done correctly, a "rollover" will not trigger taxation on the money in the plan, but if it's done incorrectly, it will.

RISK-BASED AND NON-RISK BASED TOOLS

Finally, let's take a look at the broad categories of common financial tools and understand broadly how they are typically best utilized to achieve specific income or savings goals in retirement.

"Risk-based" means that the potential gain or loss is based upon the performance of a financial market, such as the stock or bond markets; technically, these are called securities. Financial markets are volatile; meaning the value of money invested incurs both gains and losses over time, depending upon economic conditions as well as investor sentiment. Among the most commonly used forms of "risk-based" choices for retirement planning are stocks and bonds.

Stocks, of course, are ownership shares of public companies. You can invest in individual stocks, or you can invest in pools of a variety of stocks through mutual funds or exchange-traded funds. When you put your money into stocks (also called equities), you bear the "investment risk," meaning you may gain a lot or a little, or you may lose a lot or a little, either way there is no guaranteed outcome. The general advantage of stocks, whether individual or through mutual funds or exchange traded funds, is their growth potential over time; historically, stocks have proven to grow wealth over the long-term. The general disadvantage of stocks, whether individual or through mutual funds or exchange traded funds, is their loss potential. Historically stock values over the long-term increase, but when they decrease significantly, it often happens quickly and shockingly, and often unpredictably for most. The average "bear market" (a period where stocks generally lose value) only lasts for about 1½ years, but the average cumulative loss in that time -41%!

Next are bonds, which are issued by governments and corporations as a way to borrow money. While there are different types of bonds, most commonly a bond includes a rate of interest that is paid to whoever owns the bond, and at the end of the bond term (called maturity, measured in years), the amount that was borrowed is paid to whoever owns the bond at that time. The interest rate on a bond is based upon the credit-worthiness of the borrowing government or corporation; the more creditworthy, the lower the interest rate, and vice-versa. Bond ratings reflect the relative creditworthiness of the issuing government or corporation. The general advantage of bonds, whether individual or through mutual funds or exchange traded funds, is their relative stability to maintain their value. The disadvantage of bonds is their "limited liquidity" and lower potential for gains.

This means that your ability to get cash from a bond is limited to the interest payments; if you need more than that you have to sell the whole bond, you typically can't just sell as much of a bond as you need to and retain the rest of the bond.

In retirement, it is generally a good idea to have some of your portfolio in stocks, because their growth potential is needed (for most) to keep up with inflation. The exception to this is if your "emotional risk tolerance" does not allow you to sleep at night knowing that you may lose money (which is perfectly OK and acceptable by the way), or if there is no demonstrated need to achieve a high rate of return on your money. I often recommend to clients that some portion of their savings be in a portfolio of both stocks and bonds that are "actively and defensively managed" to minimize potential losses, and can shift the allocation between primarily stocks or primarily bonds as market conditions dictate.

Now a word about "Non-Risk" financial tools. In this sense, "Non-Risk" means that the potential gain may or may not be based upon the performance of a financial market, such as the stock or bond markets, but your money is protected from financial market loss. Technically, these are called insurance contracts or bank products. Money Market Accounts have traditionally been considered a "non-risk" financial choice, but this isn't really true, because there is no explicit guarantee with a Money Market Account that you cannot lose money, as many people learned in the Great Financial Crisis that occurred from 2007 to mid-2009. Amongst the most commonly used forms of "non-risk" choices for retirement planning are Certificates of Deposit and, as we discussed in detail earlier, Guaranteed Annuities.

ACHIEVING BALANCE FOR RETIREMENT

I like to say that retirement income planning is "part art and part science." The science part is all the detailed math, while the art aspect lies in the expertise and experience a strong and committed financial planner can bring to the table to help you achieve your retirement goals.

Importantly, the selection of specific financial tools (meaning the specific type of investment choices, ranging from "risk-based" choices such as stocks, mutual funds, and bonds, etc, to "non-risk" choices such as guaranteed annuities, certificates of deposit, and the like) is a matter of great debate and disagreement amongst financial professionals. Some will tell you that only "risk-based" tools are ever appropriate, while others will tell you exactly the opposite, that only "non-risk" choices are ever appropriate for retirees. Neither is completely true.

The selection of financial tools that are appropriate for your situation is not a black and white issue so be skeptical about any financial professional who seems overly dogmatic about this. There are legitimate pros and cons to any and all financial tools and investment choices. Different types of financial tools are appropriate for specific goals, and they do so with varying degrees of potential risk and reward.

At my firm, we believe that most retirees need a balance of both "risk-based" assets and "non-risk" assets to successfully navigate the potential financial challenges posed in retirement. What this balance looks like for one may be very different than for another.

This balance between "risk-based" assets and "non-risk" assets depends upon several important factors. These include the need to take a risk of loss in order to achieve a demonstrated need for a target rate of return; the amount of income produced from a financial tool relative to the principal required to produce it; the likelihood that the income produced from a financial tool is predictable, reliable, and sustainable over the long-term in both good and bad financial market conditions (and the extent that it needs to be so); and your personal tolerance for risk.

There are two equally important elements of your risk tolerance: your emotional tolerance for incurring potential losses (can you sleep at night) and your financial capacity to incur periodic losses without a devastating effect upon your security. Another major thing to consider is liquidity, or the degree to which your portfolio provides rapid access to cash, and to what extent this is likely to be necessary.

Finally—and this is a major element related to the idea of legacy that we discussed earlier—I make sure every client addresses this question: How important it is to you to leave money to your family after you are gone?

Sometimes these different factors conflict with each other, in which case it is necessary to prioritize one factor over another in order to achieve the most important goals. For example, you may want to leave money to your family, but the amount of your savings will likely only be sustainable for your retirement lifetime. Or you have little emotional tolerance for periodic losses, but in order to achieve your income goals, you will have to take some risk.

This is the value of working with a seasoned financial professional who can provide the knowledge and experience to help you maximize income while minimizing risk in your retirement planning. My personal fulfillment comes from helping clients like you navigate these sometimes-tricky waters. The goal in the end: smooth sailing towards your personal sunset!

CHAPTER 7

PLANNING FOR THE UNEXPECTED

Nothing gives me greater satisfaction than helping clients come up with a retirement plan that helps them feel more secure and in control of their future. Yet most of us know at least one person whose life and finances have been turned upside down by unforeseen illness, a bad accident, or a family emergency that changes everything, sometimes in an instant.

The discussion I have with my clients about planning for the unexpected is the one I least look forward to, but it may be one of the most crucial. It's hardly enjoyable or encouraging, but it is practical and essential–because let's face it, bad things happen to good people every day. While I never want people to worry unnecessarily, I tell them they always need to be prepared. It's no different than having car or health insurance. If life goes the way we want, we hope we never have to use it. But it's essential that we have it, and in most places, we are legally required to.

Planning for the unexpected is an integral part of retirement planning because those expenses, especially large ones relative to your total savings, can derail the so-called perfect, best-laid plan very quickly. While it's not always possible to foresee every type of unexpected expense (after all, they are unexpected), it is possible to foresee likely or probable future expenses and have a contingency roadmap for how to deal with them in a way that does not torpedo your retirement plan, and does not add undue stress to your life.

Unexpected expenses come up in a variety of ways. One issue may be the need for long-term care when a chronic health condition requires continuing assistance–something I call "The Biggie" and will discuss in detail in this chapter. Another might be an unexpected health issue that requires a lot of out of pocket spending. Yet another could be an unexpected family financial crisis (such as sudden unemployment) or even major repairs to your home that were unforeseen. Simply put, "the unexpected" generally means something that occurs that requires you to spend a large amount of money, quite often quickly, and may be ongoing for some time. This boils down to understanding that and expecting that "stuff happens" and doing what is necessary financially to be as prepared for these events as possible.

In retirement planning, your first plan is for the "known or expected" expenses such as your basic living expenses and "fun money." As we talked about in the previous chapter, this should be a budgeting and forecasting process that is very detailed. Ideally, the planning for certain potential or probably non-routine expenses are incorporated into the initial retirement income planning as well. This can include the cost of insuring against potential Long-Term Care (LTC) or other unexpected health costs by selecting the right type of insurance to minimize out-of-pocket expenses. Planning for non-health related expenses are somewhat of a challenge because in most cases, these types of expenses cannot be insured against.

LONG-TERM CARE, AKA "THE BIGGIE"

I know I usually start each chapter with a true client story, but I want to proceed here with an outside episode that I believe illustrates the importance of having a LTC insurance policy. I had a friend who worked as a nursing home administrator and he told me about a heartbreaking encounter he had with a woman who was admitting her husband for Alzheimer's disease care.

At one point in the admission process, he asked her, "How do you plan to pay for your husband's care in our facility?" She said she wasn't worried about it because Medicare would be paying the bill. When my friend heard that, he had to break the harsh news to her that Medicare would not pay for custodial care, which is the level of care her husband would be receiving in the facility. He told me he'll never forget the look on her face when she realized what he was telling her–that she would be responsible for the cost of her husband's care. It was devastating for him to hear what she told him. It was something like "The funds we have are tied up. I will need to mortgage our house to pay the nursing home bill. I'm not sure how I am going to do this, because I've never had to make any financial decisions or pay any of our bills."

This kind of scenario hit closer to home with my clients Dan and Fiona Maloosky, who didn't worry much about LTC planning until they witnessed firsthand the danger of facing their retirement years without enough savings. It broke their heart to see Dan's father struggle to care for his mother, who is in a nursing home with Alzheimer's. Dan's father, a retired teacher, had about $220,000 in savings, but it wasn't likely to be enough to pay for his wife's LTC, which ran about $70,000 a year, and carry him through retirement without government assistance.

That scenario scared Dan and Fiona, who wanted to make sure they had enough coverage so that they wouldn't face a similar plight later in life, should the worst ever happen. I was happy to help them take out an LTC insurance policy. A grateful Dan told me, "I think if my dad had done things differently, maybe purchased LTC insurance, he would be able to have in home care for my mother, which is what he really wanted. Because of what he's going through, we want to make sure we can take care of ourselves and not become a burden on our kids. So many folks think they have so much time to plan, but we learned that you have to start early."

The term "Long-Term Care" is used to describe a range of

personal care services that may be needed as a chronic health condition becomes debilitating with age. A chronic condition is a medical condition that is not expected to significantly improve, while an acute condition is one where improvement is expected. So when we talk about long-term care we're usually referring to conditions that are expected to last a lifetime. Providing personal services and care for chronic conditions is the focus of LTC. LTC services vary depending on the severity of the chronic condition, and care is delivered in a variety of settings, ranging from home health care to assisted living facilities to full-scale nursing home facilities. As you probably already know, it can cost a lot–in some cases, the equivalent of the earnings you might make from a full time job!

As I illustrated in the first scenario above, many incorrectly believe that Medicare will cover LTC costs, but Medicare only provides very limited LTC benefits, and then only under certain circumstances. Medicare Advantage plans and Medicare Supplement policies also do not provide coverage for LTC. So here's the reality: Medicare only covers medically necessary care, with a focus on acute care.

It sounds pretty black and white, but there are some gray areas. For instance, Medicare will pay for part of a short stay in a skilled nursing facility and in some cases home health care, but only if you meet the following conditions: 1) You must have stayed in a hospital for at least three days prior to needing care, and 2) You must be admitted to a skilled nursing facility within 30 days of the three day hospital stay, and 3) You must require skilled care.

If you meet these conditions, then Medicare will pay for some of your costs for up to 100 days. For the first 20 days, Medicare will pay all the costs, then for days 21 to 100 you pay all expenses up to a maximum per day, with Medicare paying the rest. After that, you pay for everything. So when we're talking about long-term care of assistance for a chronic condition, Medicare may help a bit but they generally are not going to help much.

Another key factor in play is Medicaid, which through state level programs will pay for nursing home care (but not home care or assisted living care) if you qualify due to having little assets or income. These asset and income limitations vary by state but in all cases they are very low. In some cases, it may be appropriate to do some specialty planning in order to qualify for Medicaid to pay for nursing home care, but this generally must be done well in advance of needing the care, and generally will require the services of an attorney specializing in elder law issues.

Those who need care but don't qualify for Medicaid have three choices to pay for care if they need it in the future. The first option is to self-insure. Next is to purchase a traditional long-term care insurance policy, and finally, those in need can use one of two forms of asset-based long-term care insurance. Not surprisingly, each has its pros and cons.

When you self-insure, there is no risk transfer to an insurance company. All costs will be paid from your savings. What are the advantages to self-insuring? First, you'll pay no premiums, so there's no "opportunity cost." Opportunity cost refers to the interest or earnings you would receive on the premiums you pay if you had that money invested instead of paying an insurance premium. Likewise, with self-insuring, there's no lost money if you never need care.

In other words, if you never need care, there is no lost money in the form of the total premiums you paid for insurance. The disadvantage of self-insuring is that you will bear the entire financial risk, which can lead to a very rapid depletion of your savings if care is needed for several years.

TRADITIONAL LTC INSURANCE POLICY PROS AND CONS

So now let's check out the pros and cons of purchasing a traditional LTC insurance policy. With a traditional LTC policy, you're transferring all or part of the financial risk to an insurance company, depending upon how rich a policy you can afford. The potential advantage of a traditional LTC policy is that all or most of the costs will be paid by the insurance company if you need care, which is, again, subject to the size of the policy. The potential disadvantage of a traditional policy is that the premiums can be expensive, and history tells us that the premium cost is likely to increase over time. You may incur opportunity cost on the ongoing premiums, and if you never need care, you will incur lost money in the form of the total premiums paid.

With a traditional LTC policy, in return for your premium dollars, you will get benefits, if you need them, and only for long-term care services. After you successfully pass the required medical exam, you'll pay an ongoing premium to maintain the LTC insurance policy. It breaks down pretty simply. In the future, one of two outcomes is certain: you will need care, or you will not. If you need LTC services, the traditional LTC policy will pay for care. If you never need care, the policy will expire when you do. In other words, your premium dollars will protect you if you need care, but they will provide no additional benefit to either you or your family. Despite these various limitations, I believe that a traditional LTC policy is the right option for many people.

Which leads us to that other option I mentioned, asset-based LTC insurance. With this choice, you are partially transferring the risk to an insurance company because the initial costs of care will be paid by the asset up to a limit, and then by the insurance company. The potential advantage is that your cost is largely limited to the premium or asset positioned to provide coverage if you need it. A significant potential advantage is that the structure of an asset-based solution will provide you with additional benefits if no care is ever needed, thus eliminating or reducing both opportunity cost and lost money if you never need care. The potential disadvantage of asset-based coverage is that LTC benefits will be limited by a formula and restricted to a maximum amount over time. Of course, this can also be true of traditional LTC insurance policies.

LIFE INSURANCE POLICIES AND DEFERRED ANNUITY CONTRACTS

The first of our two types of asset-based coverage is a permanent life insurance policy. With this option, you pay either an ongoing premium, or reposition a single sum of money, which creates a death benefit. As with traditional LTC insurance, as you move into the future, one of two things will occur; you will need LTC services, or you won't. If you need care, all or most of the death benefit created by the life insurance policy will be paid to you–income tax free–while you are living to pay for LTC expenses. This is typically paid to you over a period of time in monthly increments, but there are various options available.

If you need care but do not exhaust the benefit, then upon your death any remaining death benefit will be paid to your heirs income tax-free. If you never need care, then your beneficiaries will receive the death benefit upon your passing, again income tax-free. As you can see, with an asset-based type of coverage, your dollars are doing more than one thing for you, in this case providing a legacy to heirs if you don't need care, or providing the dollars for care if you need it.

The other asset-based option is a specialty type of deferred annuity contract. With this, you reposition a single sum asset that's not needed for retirement income to the deferred annuity. This creates an account value within the annuity that earns annual interest. If you need care, your account value is "leveraged" by the annuity insurer by as much as 300% to pay for LTC services, and withdrawals for qualified LTC expenses will be income tax free. Upon your death, any remaining account value, including earned interest, will be paid to your beneficiary. While you're living, you also have access to your account value for other purposes if needed. Of course, withdrawals from your account value for reasons other than LTC services may be taxable and they will reduce your future LTC benefit–so we like to think of this access as "emergency from a practical perspective."

So let's sum this up by getting back to the basic advantages and disadvantages of our choices for preventing a potential catastrophic financial event if you or your spouse needs LTC services in the future. With either the life insurance option or the annuity option, the structure provides an additional benefit to you or your family if you never need care, thus reducing or eliminating both opportunity cost and lost money if you never need care. A traditional LTC policy will only provide benefits if you need care.

Keep in mind, however, that in all cases I've mentioned, you have to qualify for the insurance coverage. Typically, the life insurance option and the traditional LTC policy choice will require medical exams, whereas the annuity option typically does not. Qualification is normally based upon your answers to basic medical questions. With all these choices, purchasing some form of protection against the costs of potential long-term care needs will decrease the chance of a catastrophic, unexpected surprise expense in your retirement.

OTHER HEALTH RELATED EXPENSES

Now let's talk about potential unexpected expenses (aside from LTC) that relate to your health. As with LTC, these can be divided between issues related to acute health surprises and chronic health surprises. We discussed the difference between "acute" and "chronic" conditions earlier, so let's talk about how to plan for those. The key to planning financially for unexpected acute conditions is medical insurance. As a retiree, you will most likely be covered under the Medicare program, specifically Medicare Part A and Part B.

Medicare Part A, called "hospitalization," is free to those who paid Medicare taxes for at least 40 quarters while working (you pay if you did not pay Medicare taxes for at least 40 quarters). Medicare Part B, known as medical insurance, charges a monthly premium based upon your income, but the vast majority of people will pay only the lowest monthly premium. Medicare Part D pays for prescription drugs and there can be a premium cost for that as well. But here's the thing: Medicare Parts A, B, and D do not pay for everything. You will have out-of-pocket costs in the form of deductibles, coinsurance, and copayments.

Although there is an annual cap on what you must pay out-of-pocket with Medicare coverage, that cap is several thousand dollars. So depending upon your retirement income and savings, you may choose to pay these out-of-pocket expenses yourself - but if you or both you and your spouse experience a significant health event, this could be a budget-buster for you.

To minimize the chance of an unexpected acute health expense, you may choose to enroll in either a Medicare Advantage Plan (Part C) or purchase a Medicare Supplement Insurance Policy. Medicare Advantage plans are offered by private insurance companies and often cover expenses not covered by original Medicare (such as dental, vision, and even wellness programs). Medicare Advantage plans may even "bundle" prescription drug coverage as well. When you enroll in a Medicare Advantage plan, there are differing price options. A basic plan may cost little more (or no more) than your basic Part B premium, which is "assigned" to the private health insurer offering the plan, whereas other options may include additional premium costs, especially those offering a larger array of benefits. With a Medicare Advantage plan, your annual out-of-pocket costs are typically lower than that for original, basic Medicare, so while you may pay more each month, you minimize the chance of a large unexpected expense.

Another option is to purchase a Medicare Supplement Policy, also known as a "Medigap" plan. Private insurance companies, in addition to your Part A and Part B coverage, offer these plans. A Medigap plan is intended to pay for part or all of the coinsurance, copayments, and deductibles, and may provide additional benefits as well, but Medigap policies do not cover prescription drugs, so you will still have to enroll in Medicare Part D for that coverage. Medigap policies also do not cover vision or dental care.

Whether you choose a Medicare Advantage plan or choose original Medicare with a Medicare Supplement policy, in both cases you are putting a likely limit upon the extent or amount of a financial surprise due to an unexpected acute medical condition. This annual limit can be built-in to your overall retirement financial plan, turning an unexpected expense into a planned expense. That's the entire key to peace of mind when it comes to those expenses we know may come up but whose specifics we can never anticipate. Finding the plan that fits you best, you have to think ahead and be prepared—so that if, heaven forbid, the worst happens, you won't have to worry about a catastrophic financial setback that throws your future off course.

PLANNING FOR OTHER UNEXPECTED EXPENSES

Some of the most common non-health related unexpected expenses that arise in retirement are major unforeseen home repairs and family assistance issues such as an adult child's sudden unemployment or divorce with which they need financial assistance. I like to call these "love issues," meaning that we can argue the issue of "personal responsibility" all we want, but quite often, the emotional impact on the retiree of a child's financial/family problem drives the train. That's just the reality sometimes—because, yes, stuff happens.

As you enter or get close to retirement, part of your planning should include identifying probable future unexpected surprises, especially with your home (assuming you are the homeowner). We often recommend that our clients have a thorough home inspection in order to identify potential future major expenses. These can include the need for a new roof or foundation or plumbing repairs. This allows you—and us as professional planners—to determine the probable future costs of the repairs, and therefore plan for those costs. This way, you turn an "unexpected surprise" into a planned expense that your financial professional can integrate into the overall plan. He or she can then help you choose the best investment choice for where to put that money until you need it. We do this routinely with our clients.

Here's a question I'd like you to think about: Can your emergency fund be invested? Of course it can, but you have to do it with caution. If you invest your emergency fund, be sure the investments are liquid, meaning that the investment can be sold (or "cashed out," if you prefer) very quickly if need be and you can obtain the cash you need within a few days or so. In some situations, it may be appropriate to keep your emergency fund money in the same investment account as your other money, so long as the investments meet the "liquidity" requirement.

However, if you prefer to be somewhat aggressive with your general investments, that may not be the best place for your emergency funds; in this case, you may want to consider a separate account that you can invest more conservatively. This is simply because money that is invested, especially aggressively, will experience ups and downs over time due to the nature of the financial markets, and you want to avoid having to withdraw money for an emergency during one of the inevitable down cycles in the investment markets if you can. Additionally, having a separate emergency account, whether held in investments or in a bank savings account, can provide emotional peace of mind. We all know how important that is to retirement professionals like me–and my clients!

CHAPTER 8

LIFE INSURANCE IS PART OF A RETIREMENT PLAN

I feel blessed to have multiple opportunities to lift the spirits of people in both my personal and professional lives. When I'm visiting schools or counseling recovering addicts who are in prison, nothing gives me greater pleasure and satisfaction than seeing the light in young people's eyes when something I have said connects with them and their eyes light up—even for a split second. In the correctional settings, I love nothing more than encouraging those folks to set their sights higher so that they never return to the depths where they've been. They know I can relate to everything they've been through, and can shine a light for them as a result. In schools, I want kids to know that there's a future with great things for them if they focus on positive values and set meaningful goals for themselves. I love giving of myself and feeling like I have made a difference.

Likewise, when I've got my suit and tie on, take a seat in the conference room and am helping clients work through the details of their ideal retirement, nothing gives me more joy than knowing that I've done something positive that will have a long-lasting impact. When it comes to choosing the right life insurance policy, the decisions I help people with are literally about life and death. Everyone knows it's important to have life insurance, but it's never a comfortable topic to bring up with couples. That's because we're literally talking about the eventual reality that one of them will pass away sometime in the coming years and leave the other one to survive not only the emotional loss, but all the resulting financial problems that could arise as well.

I usually start by telling them something like this, "We all wish our lives would always be about happy moments and happy endings, like in the movies, don't we? Let's face it; you have a lot of great years to look back on and share in the future that are really happy. But what happens when it's no longer that way? What happens when the unexpected pops up and shakes the foundation and the day-to-day things we take for granted? Are you ready for it? Because we're human beings and we're wired to survive, we have an incredible ability to tell ourselves that everything will be like a Hollywood happy ending. I wish it were otherwise, but the truth is, very few couples die on the same day. One of you will outlive the other. And when that time comes, the happiest ending you've got is the one that won't destroy you or your family financially."

Even though it's always terribly sad to lose a client who is also a wonderful person in my life, it is rewarding for me to know that by helping set up the right life insurance policy, I have helped that person's surviving spouse endure further hardship. Five years before Mr. Griffin passed away from thyroid cancer, I had helped him and his wife of 42 years take out a whole life insurance policy, which is the simplest type of permanent life insurance. With this type of coverage, the premium amount is locked in and remains the same throughout the entire lifetime of the policy. I recommended it to the Griffins because they needed to stick to a budget. Financial advisors who work with younger clients like this kind of policy too, because the client will pay the same amount when they get older, regardless of advancing age or a negative health issue. At the time, the Griffins liked the idea that the cash in this kind of policy can steadily grow, often with a minimum rate of return. Also appealing was that the policy I helped them secure was designed to provide dividends, and because it wasn't considered to be a return of premium to the policyholder, they were not taxed.

Mr. Griffin wasn't ill when they took out the policy, but within a year, he began experiencing symptoms and not long after, he had full-blown thyroid cancer and it was spreading. I was as devastated as Mrs. Griffin and their children were because everything had happened so quickly. But I'm here to shine a light on the positives from my perspective as a retirement specialist. A few months after her husband's passing, she came to my office, unannounced and with tears in her eyes, and thanked me for what I had done.

"That's my job," I said. "I'm so sorry for your loss, but I hope in some small way, I did something that is helping you and your family at least with the financial things."

She explained that when Mr. Griffin died, she was faced with a crazy list of sudden expenses: the funeral, lawyer fees for executing his estate, daily living expenses and their mortgage payments. She was also helping her children save for her teenage grandson's college tuition. If it weren't for the policy, she would have been trying to do all that with no income whatsoever, minimal job experience and savings that would have lasted only a few years.

Mrs. Griffin added that it would have been a challenge for her to get a job at her age after 15 years out of the workforce, especially in the small town outside Boston where she lived. I told her there was no shame in having no specific career to fall back on, but I was glad the money from the policy prevented her from having to consider going back to school when she was still dealing with all the other family issues. She knew life for her and her family would never be the same, but she was grateful that the money from the policy she and her husband took out would keep her going without having to worry about money for a long time.

Mrs. Griffin also told me that her gratitude had turned her into a passionate advocate for the importance of life insurance. She began telling everyone she knew that they had to get life insurance. She told them, "Figure out what monthly expenses you can cut out so that you can afford it even if you think you can't. It's much more important to have it than making sure you see the latest movies or have all the premium channels." When neighbors and friends at church asked her, she was happy to go online and tell them how affordable it was. She also made some kind referrals to me, telling folks that I had helped save her from financial ruin.

A short time later, Mrs. Griffin called me and asked me if I thought it would be a good idea to take out her own life insurance policy. In her online research, she happened upon a site called Health Markets that talked about "widow's life insurance," and she told me that she wanted to take out a policy for her grown children and grandchildren to benefit from in the event of her death. She quoted me some interesting statistics. One was about a 2013 study by the Harvard School of Public Health, which revealed that the "widowhood effect" can cause a 66 percent chance for a surviving spouse to die within three months of a spouse's death. She had passed that mark, but was still interested in taking out a policy and making her daughter the custodian of her death benefit funds. Another study by New York Life revealed that for widows whose husbands had a life insurance policy, the death benefit lasted about two and a half years–but they wished it would last for 14 years. These findings were similar to an earlier study that found that widows aged 25 and older with dependents significantly underestimated the amount of life insurance protection they needed.

"It's not just about leaving a legacy to help out my grandchildren, should they ever need it," Mrs. Griffin said. "I was thinking that as I get older, if I get sick, my daughter will probably be the one who will be my primary caretaker, and it would be nice to provide a financial cushion for her. Who knows? Down the road, she may have to help me pay my medical expenses and my cost of living needs, and this could be a financial hardship. She may have to hire outside help. My husband's cancer came on quickly, so you never know what's around the corner, and I want to make sure everyone's protected."

"I think that's a great idea," I said. "I'll look into it and you can come in and we can decide on a great policy for you."

"As soon as he died, I thought about this and thought I might be crazy," she said. "But I learned that it's a pretty common concern. From what I read, the Caregiver Action Network reported that the typical caregiver is a 49-year-old daughter taking care of her widowed 69-year-old mother. Good to cover all our bases."

LIFE INSURANCE AND HOW IT RELATES TO RETIREMENT

Life insurance is the only part of a retirement plan that actually self-completes if the retiree dies before they can fully fund their retirement plan, whether it's a 401(k), IRA, Roth IRA, SEP or any other retirement plan in the arena of self-funding retirement plans. Keeping this in mind, the life insurance plan is one of the critical components to the future of any retiree because it allows them time to build their assets in their plans–yet if they die prematurely, it provides full funding or funding to the amount of the death benefit purchased.

Here's a cool "fun fact" that puts the need for life insurance in perspective: Long before any of these modern self-funding plans were invented, life insurance policies were the original retirement plans adopted into the tax code. It's right there in Section 7702.

The value of life insurance is sometimes misdirected as a death benefit product only. That's the part most people know about, that idea that a policy will pay out a death benefit in the form of a single lump sum as a check for $1,000,000 or $250,000 depending on the amount the person purchased. In fact, that's only one aspect of a life insurance policy. The policy itself has a cash value component that can also act as a cash reserve in case of emergencies or become a supplement for their retirement income.

It's very hard to find someone who would not benefit from a life insurance contract. In fact, many people think that life insurance is not something you would ever take out on kids because they do not want to profit from the death of a child. Even that thinking is short sighted because the child may have died from a severe illness that led to significant medical bills. Along with the cost of a funeral, this could prove to be a financial hardship that would be horrible to experience on top of the mental and emotional nightmare of losing a child. From dealing with a few clients who lost young children earlier in their lives, I learned about their personal trauma and how that was just the start of a nightmare scenario that included hospital bills and time off from work and wages lost as a result. For one couple that had the foresight to have a basic life insurance policy on each of their kids, the $25,000 they received at the time of one of their deaths helped offset those financial losses.

Life insurance basically breaks down into two broad categories. The first is called term insurance or pure insurance only. Its value is the lump sum to the beneficiaries upon the death of the insured. Its premiums have a very low cost at younger ages but increases in cost as a policyholder approaches life expectancy, because the insurance company will be obligated to pay the death claim. In many cases, this type of contract will cease and not be renewed when the insured is, say, 75 or 80 and life expectancy is in the 80s.

Term life insurance is widely considered to be the most basic life insurance one can purchase, because it offers death benefit protection only, without any cash value built up within the policy over time. Many of my clients who have life insurance choose it because it's usually very affordable. With this kind of insurance, coverage is purchased for a certain length of time, say 10, 15, 20 and up to 30 years or longer. Generally speaking, the amount of the premium stays the same throughout the period that the policy is active. If the insured survives beyond the original time period designated by the policy, and he or she wants to stay covered, they will need to re-qualify for a new policy whose cost will be configured based on their current age and health status. Not surprisingly, the older one is when they renew after the initial term is over, the higher the costs are, even if the person is in relatively good health.

The other major kind of life insurance is permanent life insurance, also known as cash value life insurance. True to its name, it lasts for the policy holder's entire life, but it breaks down into its own subcategories: participating whole life, universal life, variable universal life and indexed universal life. Permanent life is different from term insurance in that it offers both death benefit protection and a cash value component. Now for a few words on the specifics on these subcategories:

With participating whole life coverage, which if you'll recall is what the clients in my earlier example took out, the premium amount is locked in and will remain the same throughout the lifetime of the policy. In some cases, where a person's pre-existing conditions require him or her to buy high risk life insurance, graded whole life policies are the only option. The cash component of this kind of policy is allowed to grow on a tax-deferred basis. In other words, the gain on the funds will not be taxed until the policyholder withdraws them. This means they can compound exponentially over the course of many years.

Universal life also provides a death benefit and cash value where funds can grow and taxes can be deferred. It's more flexible than whole life coverage because the policyholder is allowed to choose how much of his or her premium dollars will be allocated towards the death benefit, and how much will go towards the policy's cash value. The good news is, because universal life is a permanent policy, the policyholder will always have access to their cash value account.

Variable universal life builds on this concept while also allowing the policyholder to participate in a variety of different investment options such as equities. With this kind of policy, funds have a chance to grow much greater than funds in a whole life policy can. Of course, as with any market-related investment, there's potential risk as those funds are exposed to the fluctuations of the equities market. While the death benefit may rise and fall, the good news is that it will never sink below the set guaranteed amount, which is usually the original death benefit purchased at the time of application.

The last sub-category of permanent life insurance is indexed universal life. This policy gives the holder the opportunity to allocate cash value amounts to either a fixed account or an equity index account. Indexed policies offer a variety of popular indexes to choose from, such as the S&P 500 or the NASDAQ 100. Indexed universal life usually provides a downside guarantee of 1% or less, but earns potentially higher upside interest crediting, based on the performance of the chosen outside stock index. Indexed life products have a floor of zero, so a policyholder's money is always protected from downturns in the market (just like our old friend, the fixed indexed annuity!). This kind of insurance is categorized as a moderately conservative interest-sensitive life insurance product.

All of these policies have cash value as a component to them and they will be enforced to the life expectancy or beyond today. Many different combinations of these products are being offered today, so at the time of purchase, it's important to study the marketplace to determine the best policy to take out at any given time–subject to your individual needs, of course.

QUESTIONS TO HELP YOU DETERMINE THE TYPE OF COVERAGE YOU NEED

When I'm helping clients decide on the kind of life insurance coverage they need, I have a list of key questions I ask them:

- How long do you need the coverage for? Is it to cover a time of exposure like a 25-year mortgage, kid's upbringing and college years?

- Is the risk of death going to go away as a risk to covering this event, business owners with a loan or a buyout from death on a partner to their family members?

- Is this to cover your spouse or partner in the event of your death to make up for an income shortfall?

- Are you concerned about taking care of yourself if you become unable to, and how many dollars and other resources are needed to do this?

- Is this policy's value going to be used to supplement retirement funding or college funding?

After they answer these questions, the next step is determining the amount of the coverage. Not surprisingly, there are huge debates in the industry on the best way to determine this. But here's the way I go at it:

- Is it a set amount like mortgage or business loan, or it is the amount needed with some cushion of 10%?

- Is it an income replacement, i.e. pension or the loss of earnings including social security? I like to figure out the cash flow using 5% off a lump sum. A million-dollar lump sum should generate an income of $40,000 to $50,000 for life, depending on the beneficiary's age. It would increase or decrease based on their age.

- What can you afford versus what you need? Budgeting is sometimes the trickiest part, and that is the art of this business, being able to put the combination of all these elements together to craft the perfect individualized plan.

ESSENTIAL BENEFITS, DOWNSIDES AND TAX IMPLICATIONS

The true benefits of life insurance are very simple. A policy provides the cash to complete the hopes and dreams of the insured for their families, their business partners and anyone else they choose as a beneficiary, in addition to paying unexpected bills with the death of the insured. Essentially, it provides an influx of cash into an uncertain future for the beneficiaries at what is always a very difficult emotional period. I like to say, it gives them the chance to catch their breath in this time of turmoil.

The only real downside is the re-allocation of funds you once used for other expenses and fun things that will now be used for those monthly premiums. It's better to consider it an investment in the future, because you never know when your loved one will die, and it's good to have insurance for a variety of reasons at that time, not the least of which is helping keep you afloat in case you're not in a position to otherwise take care of yourself. By using the very popular chronic illness riders or long-term care riders on policies today, it's easy to argue that everyone ultimately benefits from these contracts.

As for the taxation part, the tax code is very clear on the taxation of life insurance; the proceeds from the death benefit to beneficiaries is income tax free, both federal and state. In some states, life insurance death benefits are also protected from creditors, but in other states it is not.

Over the years, I've only identified a single caveat in that if it is owned by the insured, it is included in the Estate for Estate taxes, federal and state. You can easily overcome this, however, with the increasingly high limits in the Federal Tax code that renders this a non-issue for most people. These vary by each state, so it's wise to check with a local tax attorney to see what those limits are, and to find out if the policy should be owned by an irrevocable trust to take it out of their estate.

Cash values in a permanent policy are taxed as ordinary income if the value exceeds the amount of money put into the policy. However, if the owner of the policy borrows the money out of the policy and maintains the policy for his or her entire life, no taxation will occur. This is because upon the owner's death, the proceeds of the policy pay off the loan with any leftover balance being paid out as a tax-free death benefit.

BENEFIT PAYOUTS

Life insurance death benefits are usually paid out as a lump sum very quickly, usually within 30 days from receipt of the death certificate along with their paperwork to process it. If it is clearly documented how this person died, and it's of natural causes the carrier pays it out. Extreme cases can cause delays, however. If, for example, the beneficiary murdered the insured, the insurance company would have to investigate and pay in most cases the contingent beneficiary. Beneficiaries can also elect to receive the proceeds as a lifetime income, or another specifically set period, depending on what works best for their situation–but my understanding is that 99% elect a lump-sum payment to allow them to fully control the asset.

Payments from the proceeds of a life insurance policy are paid to one or more beneficiaries designated at the time you apply for insurance. However, the owner of the policy can change or modify the beneficiaries at any time. This is because, under the tax code as stipulated, this contract is outside the rulings of the probate court as it passed the asset to whom the owner wanted it to go to, unless they named the estate as beneficiary. This is rarely recommended and is not usually in the best interest of any of the parties.

In short, the lump sum completes the retirement plan and in many policies, the death benefit serves as a chronic or long-term care benefit that takes the pressure off the remaining retirement plan to continue to grow to be used later. For advisors like me whose clients are generally older and retired or about to retire, life insurance is the foundation of many retirement plans, because they provide assurance that the rest of the plan will be completed in the event of an untimely death or unexpected time of disability.

CHAPTER 9

ESTATE PLANNING AND ASSET DISTRIBUTION

As you know by now, one of my favorite parts of being a financial advisor specializing in retirees is educating clients about all of the issues I've been discussing in this book. I love shedding light, dispelling myths and sharing the knowledge and wisdom I've accumulated over my many years of helping people achieve their retirement goals and dreams. Because we live in an age where search engines allow everyone to become something of a "five minute expert" on so many topics, it's more common in 2018 for clients to come in with research they've done on various aspects of retirement plans, which they want me to look over and discuss.

The one area that almost everyone I meet knows a bit about, even without detailed Googling, is estate planning–in part because we live in a celebrity obsessed culture where the goriest details of the lives of famous people come at us through a multitude of media every day. Still, one of the most famous celebrity estate horror stories long pre-dates the 24/7 news and social media era we're in now.

Simply put, "Estate Planning" ensures that upon your passing, your assets are left to whom you want, when you want, and how you want. In other words, estate planning sets forth exactly how you want your assets distributed when you no longer need them since, as we all know, you can't take it with you.

Estate planning is done to ensure that your wishes regarding your family and other concerns (such as charitable passions) happen the way you want them to, with the least possible delay and difficulty. For people with a lot of assets, estate planning can also be critical in minimizing the impact of taxes when your assets are transferred after your death. Estate planning can also give you "control from the grave" if you have heirs that are poor money managers and you want to place restrictions on when or how they can access or spend their inheritance–or you have children with special needs and want to be sure that they are protected after your death. If you are married, estate planning can also play an important role in ensuring that your surviving spouse is taken care of as you would want, and with the least time and burden imposed by the "legalities" of transferring property.

Before detailing what constitutes your "estate" and how this planning is done, first let's look at what can happen without estate planning.

Jimi Hendrix is one of the greatest guitarists in history and one of the most famous musicians of the 20th century. When he died on September 28, 1970, he had no will, leaving his estate and the right to his music under the control of the court for the next 25 years. After suing, Jimi's father, Al, won the legal right to his son's estate and music in 1995. Yet, when Al passed away in 2002, he left his son's $80 million estate under the sole control of Jeanie, his adopted daughter from another marriage. By doing this, he basically disinherited the relatives that Jimi was closest to during his life. Not long after Al's death, Jimi's brother sued Jeanie over the rights to Jimi's estate, resulting in years of lawsuits.

I won't sugarcoat this. When someone dies without an estate plan, their survivors are left high and dry to deal with the resulting chaos and conflict in courts and family–especially when there's a huge fortune on the line. In Hendrix's case, his failure to create a will deprived the world of his music and his relatives of inheriting his estate.

Another famous rock and roll estate plan fiasco was Elvis Presley. The King failed to make proper legal arrangements to distribute his estate, which means that a large amount of his assets went through a probate process. Because of the lengthy and expensive process, his estate was reduced by over 70%–which hopefully it's made back over the years because Elvis is still one of the highest earning dead celebrities. Still, his family had to pay millions of dollars in taxes, fees and legal costs.

Not leaving a will is bad, but equally troublesome complications can arise when someone leaves behind a will that hasn't been updated in years. A more recent celeb case I remember was actor Heath Ledger. When he died in 2008, he left a will that had not been updated since 2003. Since his will was written before the birth of his daughter, it left everything to Heath's sister and parents. To the dismay of the actor's family members, the conflict over the will played out over the media, with all the crazy details and feuding on display for all the world to see.

The most recent celebrity case, and one of the most tragic, is that of Prince, who left behind a $300 million estate when he died in April 2016. Since the pop legend didn't plan his estate, his family and loved ones are stuck with the nightmare of probate proceedings. Between the current federal estate tax rate of 40% and an additional 16% from the state of Minnesota, the majority of Prince's estate is going to pay taxes. From everything I have read about the case, there are many things that could have been done to avoid probate and minimize estate taxes. I suppose when an artist is still creatively active and relatively healthy at 57, he may have thought he had years to worry about it–but as we have discussed throughout this book, life doesn't always give us that option.

Prince had many longtime friends and reportedly stayed close to both of his former wives. Sadly for them, none will get any of his estate, which instead is subject to claims from a variety of relatives with whom Prince shared little, if any, connection.

He could have avoided this circumstance by creating a trust to benefit those close to him.

Making these kinds of poor decisions and blunders is something that everyone from the rich and famous to the average working person in America does. None of my clients are celebrities, but many have told me estate planning horror stories about people they had known. I was pleased that they came to me to avoid the kinds of nightmares they felt free to share with me. Mr. and Mrs. Lieber sat down at the conference table and told me about a friend they had whose father had remarried years after his first wife passed away. The father had recently retired when he suddenly fell ill and required hospitalization. He died a week later. He had no will, and at that time in Massachusetts, the law stated that the current spouse got everything.

"The kids were left with nothing," Mrs. Lieber added, "and the new widow was really anxious about having enough money to live on for the rest of her life, so she would not disclaim any of the inheritance. You can guess what happened. The widow and the children didn't speak to each other for years."

Just as I was absorbing that story, Mr. Lieber jumped into the conversation with another one. "We knew this man who was a successful business owner with a $4 million dollar estate. He died at 64 but had no will, wasn't married and had no kids. So that left his nine brothers and sisters to wrangle over these assets. We ran into one of his brothers and he told us that the family had always been somewhat dysfunctional but the case dragged on and brought out the worst in all of them. We later found out it took nearly two years to close the estate."

EXPLAINING ESTATE PLANNING AND ASSET DISTRIBUTION

Before detailing the process and legal tools used in estate planning, I would like to explain exactly what constitutes your estate, and what happens upon your death without estate planning. Simply put, your estate is everything that you own when you die–your cash, investments, retirement accounts, house, cars, collectibles and all other possessions, including any ownership interest in a small or closely held business. Different types of property and accounts pass to heirs in differing ways and with differing tax treatments, some more complex than others, and estate planning can streamline and, in some respects, simplify the process overall.

Many people mistakenly believe that if they do no estate planning, and even if they do not write a basic will, that all of their property will automatically pass either to their spouse or their children. While this may be the eventual outcome, when you die without a will, you are considered to have passed away "intestate." This means that the laws of your state (these laws differ among states) determine the distribution of your property. This in most cases will be a time-consuming process, one in which you will have no say, and the outcome may differ dramatically from what you would prefer. Generally, these state laws are going to trigger a process called "probate."

Actually, even if you have a written will, but no other estate planning documents, the probate process may also be triggered, since the definition of probate is "the official proving of a will."

THE PERILS OF PROBATE

Probate is the court-overseen process of proving the validity of a will, determining an estate's value, identifying and paying creditors from the estate, and distributing the estate property to the heirs. The potential problems that I refer to as the "perils of probate" are:

- **Time:** In most (if not all) cases, this can take several months, and if you have a lot of assets, it can take over a year or even many years if potential heirs and creditors decide to contest your will. For example–to bring up yet another famous case–the singer James Brown died in 2006 and left his estate to charities. His heirs disputed his will and the case has still not been settled. There are many similar examples like this.

- **Expense:** Probate involves attorney fees and court fees, and may also include other expenses such as appraiser costs and even executors fees. It is not unusual for these costs to consume 5% of the estate's value, sometimes more if the estate is large and heirs or others contest the will.

- **Public Exposure:** The probate process is a public process. The process allows literally anyone to make a claim on your property, and the validity of any claim has to be determined by the court. This cannot only take time, it can add to the overall expense as well. There is also no privacy involved; anyone can find out exactly what you left behind, and who ultimately inherited what.

The probate process can also have a devastating emotional impact upon your family if disputes arise amongst the family or other heirs named in your will, or if you have no will and die intestate. This potential impact of probate can linger and cause resentment long after the estate is settled.

Some types of property pass to heirs without the probate process, with or without a will or other estate planning documents. These include any property held in a trust; jointly-owned property (but not common property); life insurance death benefits, unless they're payable to the estate; any property you give away before you die; cash or equivalent assets held in a "Pay on Death" account such as a bank or brokerage account that has been designated as such; and retirement accounts such as an IRA or 401(k) with a named beneficiary.

For most people, particularly those that own a house or other property and have modest savings, it is generally a good idea to do some estate planning, especially if they want to ensure that upon their death, their property is distributed to whom they want, when they want, and how they want.

THE BASICS OF ESTATE PLANNING

For most people, especially those whose estate is not likely to exceed $5.45 million including any life insurance death benefits (triggering potential federal Estate Tax), estate planning is generally fairly simple and affordable. While there are many versions of "do it yourself" kits available for estate planning, it is advisable to use a competent attorney to prepare your estate planning documents. Any attorney specializing in estate planning will be able to ask you questions that may not occur to you, and assure that your estate planning documents accurately reflect your intentions.

The cornerstone documents of a basic estate plan are:

- **Last Will and Testament:** This document details who inherits your property, but as we discussed previously, a will is contestable and triggers the probate process.

- **A Trust:** A trust is simply a legal entity that holds property and sets forth the terms and rules for managing the property and ultimately distributing the property. There are many different types of trusts (some of the basics are covered later in this chapter), but the two key things are that property held in a trust is not subject to probate, and generally the instructions for distributing property held in a trust cannot be challenged in court after your death. Therefore trusts, whether simple or complex, are widely used in estate planning. If your property is held in a trust, then it is common for your will to simply state that your property will be distributed according to the instructions detailed in the trust.

- Powers of Attorney and Health Care Directives: These important documents specify who makes financial and health care decisions for you if you become incapacitated. This typically includes a living will, which specifies your wishes in regards to your healthcare.

TRUST ME!

Many people mistakenly believe that trusts are only for "the rich," but this is far from true. Trusts are commonly used in estate planning for those of modest means, because they avoid probate and therefore the "perils of probate" discussed earlier in this chapter. While there are many types and variations of trusts, some of the most common types of trusts are:

- **Revocable Living Trust:** The most common trust in estate planning, this one is established to hold ownership of property such as real estate, savings or investment accounts (but not retirement accounts such as IRA or 401(k), and other assets. When the trust is established, ownership of the property is transferred to the trust, and the trust specifies how, when, and to whom that property will be distributed at your death. The trust also specifies who manages the property while you are living (this is usually you as the "trustee"), and who will function as the "successor trustee" after your death to ensure that the distribution happens according to your wishes. As the name implies, this type of trust is revocable, meaning that you can remove property from the trust and make other changes while you are living.

- **Irrevocable Living Trust:** This is used to move assets from your ownership to trust ownership, typically for passage to heirs at your death. In most cases, an irrevocable trust is only used when your estate is likely large enough to trigger estate taxes, and therefore the trust is established while you are living to reduce the value of your estate upon your death. This ensures that the trust will avoid or reduce estate tax liability. As the name implies, this type of trust is irrevocable, meaning that once property is transferred to the trust, this cannot be changed later. There are a lot of variations of irrevocable trusts.

- **Special Needs Trust:** This is used to provide assets to care for a physically or mentally disabled beneficiary. This can be done to make sure that the beneficiary remains eligible for government benefits, or to provide specific instructions for how an asset will be managed and paid-out for the benefit of the beneficiary.

- **Generation-Skipping Trust:** Used to transfer substantial assets tax-free to beneficiaries who are at least two generations after you–typically grandchildren.

There are many more types of trusts, but those I have listed above should give you a good idea of how trusts can be used to benefit your family or other heirs after your death. I think it's important that you consult with an attorney to determine what type of trust is appropriate for your situation and desires.

ESTATE PLANNING QUESTIONS

As we work with clients, we also work hand-in-hand with attorneys to determine the best estate planning tools for them. In doing so, we ask a lot of questions that seem obvious to the client, and others that trigger a "Wow, I had not thought of that" response. For example, for clients who will not likely incur estate taxes (this includes most Americans), we help identify their desires for property distribution amongst their family members with questions such as:

Do you want your real estate holdings to be kept in the family, or would you prefer that they are sold and the proceeds distributed to your heirs? What if one of your children wants to keep the house or other real property? If so, should their share of other property be reduced proportionally, or should they purchase the property from your estate?

Do you have a vacation home with lots of family memories that you want to remain available to all of your children? How will ownership be established, and who should be responsible for maintenance?

Do you want to divide your assets equally amongst your children, or are there reasons why you would prefer an unequal distribution? Do you have any children with special needs that will require help in managing their inheritance?

Is there anyone besides your children that you want to leave property or assets to?

Do you own a business, and if so, how do you want your ownership in the business to be distributed at your death? Are any of your children involved in the business? If so, do you want them to inherit a larger share of the business, or do you want to specify who will manage the business on behalf of other heirs?

Do you have any personal items or collectibles that you want to specify are left to a specific child or grandchild?

Upon your death, but before your spouse's death, do you want to distribute a portion of your assets or property to your children or grandchildren?

Do you want to leave assets or property to a charity or church that is important to you?

I think by now you get the point. Thinking about these things and deciding what you want to happen is integral to the estate planning process. Based upon the answers to these and other questions, the proper estate planning documents and specific language within those documents can be completed.

Your estate distribution desires can also impact your overall retirement plan, because they can impact the type of financial tools used to preserve, grow, and generate income from your savings. Therefore your estate planning needs and goals are a key component in overall retirement planning. Ideally, it should be an integrated process.

The key impact of estate planning is that, when done properly and with the right tools, you are able to think about these important matters now while you are living, and then guarantee that your intentions and desires at your death are very clear. This not only simplifies and speeds up the distribution of your assets at death, but can also avoid potential conflicts amongst your heirs like the kind James Brown, Elvis, Prince and Jimi Hendrix left behind along with their musical treasures. Simply put, estate planning is an act of love. It ensures that those you love and care about will inherit your property quickly and without conflict, and in the manner you desire.

CHAPTER 10

A MESSAGE OF HOPE

I am aware that most books about the financial industry and retirement planning stick to the brass tacks of explaining concepts and strategies, but as you know if you've read this far, to me that is only half of my story. Believe me, I truly love educating people on the important concepts that I've covered in this book, from "The Two ROIs" to "Maximizing What you Already Have" to "Estate Planning and Asset Distribution." As much as I pride myself on being a strong strategist when it comes to helping people with their nest eggs, I consider education an equally crucial part of the job. I love when clients come to me having found some answers on the Internet, but I enjoy it even more when they come in with questions. Nothing is quite as fulfilling in my profession as that moment of breakthrough, where the light bulb goes off and they have clarity on an issue that previously confused them.

After many chapters sticking to discussions of financial issues, the reason I call this final chapter "A Message of Hope" is because it illustrates my belief that faith can move mountains–if we bring a shovel. It captures the feeling that with discipline and spiritual growth, God can use even the most broken people to contribute to society and bless others–as I have had the opportunity to do. Hope to me is that flicker of light that keeps you going when you're at the bottom. That glimpse of something beyond yourself, that makes you think maybe, just maybe, there is a God or Spirit of the universe that will carry you through. I know it may seem unusual to some that someone with my financial background would delve so deeply into spirituality in a book whose subtitle, after all is, *Protect Your Wealth and Create Reliable Income for a Happy and Secure Retirement*. Yet, I believe my personal spiritual definition of hope ties in perfectly with the more earthbound hope that I want to bring my retirement clients when we talk about the rest of their lives.

I want to brighten their future. I want them to know that it's not about them or me that makes things come together. It's about "we." It's about the energy that comes from us working together in a positive manner that makes it work and enlivens and illuminates the great possibilities of that future.

One of the things I've really enjoyed about writing this book has been starting each chapter with a personal encounter with a client that relates to the topic I will be discussing. I have done that to showcase not only my essential process, but to demonstrate that above all else, my clients matter to me. People matter to me as individuals, and their concerns become my concerns. Maybe there are some retirement counselors who care more about crunching numbers and discussing policy. Those details matter, but for me, personal interactions drive everything I do in this business.

In the spirit of those chapter-opening encounters, I will open here with a story not about a client at the office, but someone I have dedicated myself to bringing hope to in my other life as a counselor. I had a young man from my jail program named Johnny (we call him "Johnny" out of respect for his privacy and anonymity) who had spent 17 of his 34 years in jail–half his life. He came from a family riddled with drugs, prison stays and alcoholism. He grew up surrounded by hopelessness and despair, and felt that the cards were stacked against him from the start. I certainly can't take all the credit, but I know our discussions, my encouragement and being able to share my story of redemption has helped him tremendously. He's now a productive, working member of society who finds great fulfillment speaking to young kids about the dangers of drugs and alcohol. Everybody can read about those dangers, but until you hear a first person encounter, and about one person's road to hell and back, it's all pretty abstract.

Another great guy I know I helped was Fred (again, not his real name) who had done time for theft and screwed up his life in so many other ways that the robbery was just a small aspect of his so-called spiritual rap sheet. Today, he's a husband and father, owns a construction business and helps many addicts by giving them work and getting them clean.

PAST EXPERIENCES INFLUENCE THE PRESENT

I believe that my past experiences influence everything I do in the here and now, especially for my clients. This is because I am very grateful for receiving another chance, and I want to give 100% to everything I do. Every day, I lament the fact that I missed out on so much of life for so many years. If you'll remember in Chapter Two, I talked about promising God that if He gave me another chance, I would never take a moment, chore or small task for granted.

Some of my newer clients who don't yet know my story may not be aware of it, but they, like those who know me well, personally benefit from all of my personal experiences, trials and triumphs over the dark days. Every qualified financial advisor worth their salt should be fully committed to those who trust them with their future, but I take that concept further as a way to pay everything forward and show appreciation. My clients receive service and guidance that exceeds anything they could get elsewhere.

Most advisors at my level work maybe 9 a.m. to 4 p.m. three to four days per week, spend summers vacationing at the beach and enjoy much of the winter hundreds of miles south of here in tropical climates. That's great for them, but it's just not my style. I feel like I missed out on a lot of life in many ways, and I am grateful. Gratitude is an action word as I'm sure I've said before, and I show it by working six days a week to ensure that I'm present for my clients whenever they need me. I only vacation when my mentor forces me to because he fears I may start burning out.

Sometimes I think about how different my career in the financial industry might have been had I never been an addict or been redeemed. I think it's likely that I would have ended up like most advisors that run their businesses in a more formal, less social fashion, doing only the bare minimum of what is necessary for clients rather than offer the deep level of personal service that has become part of my trademark mission. Let's face it, for most advisors it's a job or a means to make money and enjoy a certain lifestyle. For me, it's a passion. It's my purpose. It's who I am. It's how I fulfill my role on earth.

FEELING OF SECURITY AND CONFIDENCE

Another thing I believe is that everyone I work with should feel secure and confident no matter what happens down the line. I think what sets me apart from other advisors is that I pray for each client before each meeting, asking God to allow me to be of service to that person or those people first and foremost. I spend hours with clients so as to better understand them, who they are, their needs and how I can best serve them. If I ever feel that there is someone else who could better serve those specific needs, I will refer them to that professional. Because it's not about me, it's about making sure my client's needs are met. I refuse to pound a square peg into a round hole. At the end of the day, it's between me and God, not me and them.

There are four different ways that I give my clients a feeling of security when they are working with me. I have weaved these throughout this book, but for emphasis, I would like to summarize them again here. First, I analyze where they are right now and what their needs will be in the future. To do this, I ask them questions to find out their expenses (needs and wants), factor in inflation, use strategies to maximize Social Security, identify income gaps and determine sources of savings to close gaps.

Second, I find secure, guaranteed sources of income through annuities and through maximizing SS and pensions. Again, we use strategies to maximize Social Security and pensions using an insurance technique to get maximum income while protecting their spouse. We use annuities with incline riders to fill in the difference between a client's income goal and what they have coming in month to month to close that gap with guaranteed predictable income for life that keeps pace with inflation and is not subject to stock market risk.

Third, we prepare for the worst with Disability, Life and Long-Term Care insurance. As I explained in previous chapters, we use life insurance for a few reasons–tax-free income, death benefit to cover estate taxes and long-term care protection. Finally, I am committed to guaranteeing my clients' legacies through Estate Planning and Asset Distribution. We use life insurance to ensure that a person's estate isn't depleted due to nursing home care. It's important to ensure that all estate tax and other obligations are met.

NO MATTER YOUR PAST, GOOD THINGS CAN HAPPEN IN YOUR FUTURE

I have a one word response for people who ask why I believe that no matter where you've been or where you are in life, and how bad those things may be or have been, good things can happen in your future: Faith! Faith believes in things not yet seen. Some folks say, "I'll believe it when I see it," but I focus on visualization and positivity and KNOW that if I believe it in my heart and hold a vision of it as true, I will receive it. Other opinions don't matter. It's a fact.

I have learned from experience that the ability to overcome terrible adversity can result in an outlook more positive than you could ever imagine. Once you've been through hell and found a POWER that can help you overcome anything. You will understand that problems are simply growing blocks on the way to a better future. Adversity is what makes or breaks us. It's how we respond that makes all the difference. The reality is that the hammer that smashes glass molds steel. It all comes down to what you are made of. The bottom is a springboard to the top.

Let's face it, no matter how positive our outlook is overall, we all have our moments of doubt. We all find ourselves slipping into a negative mindset based on the next crisis on our plates. The way I work my way out of these is by affirmations. I talk to myself positively all the time. Think about it. Who do you listen to more than yourself? We're always telling ourselves stories about each situation. They're often negative unless we're in the right mindset. So I train myself. I want to be in shape mentally and physically. I work out every day at 5 a.m. and eat healthy. So if I want my mind to be healthy, I need to train it. I have a positive mind training routine every morning. I wake up at 4:30 a.m. to pray, read positive words, sayings or Biblical passages, meditate, do affirmations and visualizations, get to the gym by 5:15 a.m, bring coffee home to my wife by 6:15 a.m, then start my day.

FINAL POINTS AND THANK YOUS

If you're uncertain about retirement, I'm here to help. Remember, hope is not a plan. I've learned in life that it's crucial to take an honest, solid look at where you're headed, where you're trying to get to and how on track you are. It's imperative that you are involved with a third party with experience because we humans have a funny way of lying to ourselves in our own voices. Without the proper guidance, we often just cosign our own nonsense.

In both financial and personal matters, there are always options available to you. It's never too late. Never. If you're breathing, you still have a chance. I don't care at what point you're at, the elevator is going down and it's your choice what floor you want to get off on. That's how I look at the choice between staying an addict and committing to recovery. And that's one of my philosophies of life.

So many people came into my life when I needed them, and this is my time to pay it forward by helping as many people as possible, whether it is through my work with retirees or through my counseling and other charitable activities. As of now, we're trying to use my organization The Ryan Fund to help veterans, folks in church that are in need, help addicts get into treatment and help pay for an education for kids whose families have fallen on tough times–especially if the family nucleus has fallen apart or if addiction played a role.

My hope is that everyone who reads this book understands that there is an all–powerful Presence operating in this world and that Power or Presence is available to each of us at any time. I'll say it again; it's never too late. And as long as our goals are aligned with that Source of love, nothing is impossible through that Source that strengthens me.

This may strike some of you as odd, but I believe in taking a holistic approach to every relationship in life. I realize that whether I'm working with a client, an addict I'm trying to help, or spending time with my spouse, or amazing five-year-old stepdaughter, there should be one common bond between everyone–that thing that makes us one. Forget the physical body or the role of being the advisor, sponsor, husband, or stepdad. For that moment, it should be about that oneness. In the big picture, we are all one and when we work as one, EVERYONE benefits–the client and advisor, the sponsor and "sponsee," the wife and the husband, the stepdaughter and stepfather.

The money, my business, the good press I have received...these are all gifts I enjoy, but today my life is filled with real treasures. One is my recovery crew that are strong, solid honest men of integrity who are always there walking the walk with me. I also have many friends who are not in recovery but who choose to live the right way day in and day out. Every day I get to enjoy amazing client relationships. It's been said that people spend 40-50% of their life working, and it's such a gift to have clients that enhance my life and who I look forward to seeing every day. Most people dread it when Mondays come around. I actually look forward to going to work each day…such a gift. I've been blessed with the wisdom to keep in mind that there are two pains in life–the pain of discipline and the pain of regret. I know the pain of regret from all those years ago and refuse to feel that ever again.

I was blessed with two solid parents. Nobody fought harder for my life than those two. Words can't express how grateful I am. I'm also fortunate enough to have a great friendship with the deacon at my church. Frank, and St. Patrick's church, have helped had Amanda and me immensely.

Last, but definitely not least, I feel so blessed to be married now to the girl of my dreams (mentally, physically, and most of all spiritually), Amanda. I lost her 12 years ago due to my poor choices and to have her back is the ultimate dream come true–the last piece of the puzzle I was fortunate enough to recover.

An added bonus is the special connection I have with her daughter, Kennedy. I never thought I'd be doing ponytails, but the two days a week I drive her to school, I do them (and I'm getting pretty good at it). We also have a very spirited bulldog named Ted. We are hoping to add a little baby to the mix. I wake up by 4:30 a.m. next to Amanda, and roll out of bed onto my knees and I pray. On the days Amanda works, I go out to get us coffee so we can have coffee together before she leaves at 5:30 a.m. People often ask, "Isn't it hard getting up to go get coffee that early?" My reply is "Yes, but the payoff is that I get to spend a few minutes starting my day with someone as special as Amanda." I always remind myself that I would've walked on hot coals for the chance to go fetch her coffee at 4:45 a.m when we weren't together. She's amazing. Then I make the bed. I do that because it's all about the little details–how you do one thing is how you do everything.

Then I get little Kennedy ready for school and we either have breakfast at home or I take her for breakfast nice and early so we can go to the playground before school. I cherish my time with her. She's such a special little girl. On the days Amanda doesn't work, I go to the gym in morning, and afterwards I usually go with Amanda to drive Kennedy to school.

I then go to work and my day just keeps getting better, because I love my job. I have an amazing support team that works behind the scenes for me and I am at a level that I can pick and choose what clients we take so I am blessed to be of service to some great folks.

My day is always busy (some say crazy) and my appointment book is stacked full. Some days I'll cut out and pick up Kennedy from school, which always reminds me what's important. She comes to work and uses my office as her own! My wife, my stepdaughter and parents are always popping in here.

Often, if you stop by my office, a client might be sitting here because "they were in the area and thought they'd pop in for coffee." I love that. I love that clients feel that at home here, and that's because I truly love my clients. I believe "gratitude" is an action word, so I do things to show them. Some things are small, such as always calling them back right away, or calling just to say hi or check in on them. Other things are bigger, like reaching out to make any adjustments that might be necessary, or giving clients tickets to games or events. This year, we are hosting a very classy client appreciation event that clients are allowed to bring a friend (so they feel comfortable and enjoy their dinner). This event is very high end. "Why spend money on your business that isn't going to make you money? Other advisors have asked me this many times. It's not about money, it's not about business. It's about gratitude.

I end the day the way I started it with my best friend and soul mate as we do a gratitude workbook. We read a book called *The*

Magic and incorporate gratitude and prayer in our nightly ritual. We are blessed. I usually work until 8:30 at night, whether I'm seeing a client or conducting a workshop. We teach retirement workshops and seminars and have had a tremendous amout of success. Other advisors constantly bombard us, and larger firms ask us to teach and show them how we did it. My attorney, John, and my close friend (who is like a brother), Joe, suggested that I copyright my process and allow advisors and firms to buy my workshop.

So, we are now in the process of launching Diamond Advisory Systems (DAS), which allows other advisors that want to become retirement specialists and build a strong, successful retirement practice information on my process. This is also geared toward folks from other walks of life that would like to become a financial advisor focusing on retirement planning, but don't know where to start to break into the industry and have an instant impact. We brand the seminar to them, teaching them how to give a seminar, but we go further, giving them a copy of the "fact finder" or chart we use to gather information during the first meeting and teach them how to run a meeting.

After that, we show them how to put together a report that shows exactly what the client needs to do in order to ensure guaranteed income for life and it helps the advisor to be sure they're doing the right thing by the client and not just selling them. Then we teach them how to continue to grow while servicing existing clients and we offer biannual one on one business coaching. I love mentoring advisors. I was motivated to do this out of frustration because there are so many advisors that aren't retirement specialists and would take on a client 20 years old, 35 years old, 55, 64, and 72 years old. NOBODY can know how to deal with all that! You wouldn't want your eye doctor doing heart surgery, right? Same thing. So I want to change the culture and create a different generation of advisors...a generation that wants to help the baby boomers undergo this dramatic transformation from accumulation to distribution the "right way."

Whatever God gives me is a blessing beyond what I ever thought I would have or could ever feel I deserve. He has surpassed my wildest dreams already. Thank you to the Creator (who I choose to call God).

One final thought as I thank you for reading my book and getting to know me on a personal and professional level through its pages. I implore you to never give up, never quit, hold your vision in the front of your mind and please pray. At first, you may think you're praying to something you don't understand, but as I have always liked to say, "Just believe that I believe."

Life is truly good, amazing actually, as long as I pray, meditate, and live it on spiritual terms. The journey continues, and I can't wait to see what tomorrow brings. And the next day. And the next...

ACKNOWLEDGEMENTS

*Everyone needs PCP (Push, Connection, Pull)

*God, my life has been like a long example of the "Footprints" poem... at different phases of my life God has put people in my path and worked in them to carry me when I wasn't strong enough to walk...

The people who have pushed me...

First, without a doubt, my mom. Nobody has done more for me... Mom, you raised me the right way and the greatest gift you gave me was God and faith. The Mother Teresa prayer resonates in my mind with you saying, "At the end of the day Ted, it's between you and God, not between you and them."

Dad, you are an example of what a man should be. If I can be half the husband you are, I'll consider myself a success. Thank you for pushing me to be a man of integrity.

Lindsay, I'm very grateful for all of your support–each day I would receive a funny card while in jail...everyone looked forward to it.

Billy, thank you for taking the values that were instilled in my life years ago, that I lost as I fell into the hell of addictions, and awakening and cultivating them as you awakened my spirit. I'll never be able to put into words what you've done for me, but I'll spend my entire life trying to pay it forward.

Dan, "we're a team." When asked why I never gave up on you, I say, "Because there's something special about that kid..." Back then, I saw a good kid in you...boy did it pay off. When I was at my lowest, the lowest I had been since rebuilding my life, I turned to you. However, that "good kid" had grown into a remarkable young man, and God worked through and with us as you walked me through the book Resilience. We would review what I read every night, and you would spend hours on the phone with me as I got back on track. Thank you...I love you, my little brother.

Jimmy, I can't express what a miracle you are. You have grown into the man that God meant you to be. We strengthen each other–steal sharpens steal.

David, it's amazing that we might go weeks without talking (other than text), but when one of us needs the other, we're just a call away.

Shawn, both you and David have become family...I love the texts we exchange each morning–we don't go this way alone... each of us needs all of us.

Artie (Welcome) What happened at that men's step meeting on your porch years ago changed me forever on a personal and spiritual level.

Artie Clark, It's funny how we only speak probably twice a month, yet you have had, and continue to have, such a profound impact on my relationship with God. In addition, I greatly appreciate you handling all of my client's mortgage needs.

The original DMOV crew, that bond was–and always will be–special.

Vinny Piro, thank you for making decisions for me that I was not capable of making for myself years ago. Today, I'm grateful for your friendship and I value our java meetings at your office...

Michael Higgins, you were beyond hard on me, but you were fair–and in the end, you vouched for me in a way that enabled me to live the life I have today.

Brian Donahue, thank you for helping me over the years to build an amazing retirement practice allowing me to help so many folks to protect their nest egg and enjoy the life they deserve. The support I have received from you and your team has played a profound role in allowing SFP to get to this level.

Bobby Rufo, Captain of the Woburn Police Department, thank you for always treating me with respect and dignity; and for being a supportive friend throughout my comeback.

Bob Ferullo, Chief of the Woburn Police Department, thank you for all you do to help those that are suffering in Woburn. I'm grateful to know you.

John Truelove, you always found a way to ensure that my practice was sheltered from negativity, and as long as I lived "right" you assured me things would be "ok," and we would "get through it."

Joey A., I'm grateful to have you in my life, brother. Whether we're talking family, business, or golfing, we always have a great time together.

Dr. Peltz, thank you for helping me to find the middle ground of balance.

Jon Illig, thank you for taking the time to teach me how to give workshops. I'm beyond grateful for your contribution to this work and my practice as a whole. I'm also blessed to have you as a friend.

All the folks at DNA and CelebrityPress® that made this book possible...you took my vision and made it a reality...Thank you.

My business coach, Greg Rollett, thank you for implementing the perfect day process in my life...you have helped me put so many processes together that have improved my life immensely... and thank you for making me accountable.

My connection:

I believe it's crucial to have a connection to something greater... I'm so grateful for my connection with God and those who have enabled me to feel God's presence and/or be a conduit of His love...I named my business "Summit Financial Partners" after reading *The Power of Positive Thinking* by Norman Vincent Peale. He said, "Make God your business partner in everything you do." Right then, Summit Financial Partners was born.

Steve Biagioni, thank you for allowing me to start a freshman night for the kids and their parents in order to speak to them about making the right decisions.

Serge Clivio, thank you for the opportunity to come in and work weekly with your "business ethics" class, allowing me to guide your students on building a professional future built on ethics and values.

Father Mario, I appreciate the way you've managed to bridge the gap between who I am and my past, enabling me to feel at home at church.

Deacon Frank, you have had an impact on not only me, but also on my wife, Amanda, and daughter, Kennedy. You have brought God to our home and made the church our second home. Thank you for marrying Amanda and me, and guiding us on our path of marriage. Thank you for allowing Amanda and me to donate and help so many that are in need. We love you.

Sandy Allan, of Woburn Counsel on Concern, thank you so much for allowing me, my business and Amanda to be of service to those folks who are in need.

Anthony Fontana, of St. Pat's School, thank you for allowing me to give back to the school my little one attends.

Thank you to the folks at C.A.P. Reflections, for giving me a solid foundation as I started my recovery there. I'm especially grateful for the opportunity to go back and start a workshop for the men there who are trying to overcome obstacles and rebuild their lives.

Ed Bleu, thank you for bringing Dan and me into the jail to start what proved to be a life changing group for both the inmates as well as Dan and I.

And lastly, my pull...

My amazing wife, Amanda, you are my pull. I am so grateful to start each day looking at the girl of my dreams. I believe that love is the strongest of all emotions, and once I found it, love suddenly changed everything. I want to be my best and provide for my family, including little Kennedy, who I couldn't love more.

They say, "Behind every good man is a good woman..." I can honestly say that you're behind the scenes in every area of my life. You make me so much better than I ever was on my own.

My clients, you are the reason I have the life I have...I strive each and every day to become better for you folks. I want to truly make your life better than it would be without me. I can honestly say that over the years my clients have evolved into friends and more so family. The summit financial family is one that is based on gratitude. I believe gratitude is an action word and rather than say I'm grateful, I try to show it. You folks are such a blessing.

About Ryan

A trailblazer in the field of asset preservation and distribution, retirement specialist Ryan Skinner—co-owner of the Woburn, MA based firm Summit Financial Partners—sets the standard for developing long-lasting personal relationships with his clients. He is driven by his passion to help people achieve "worry free" financial independence with solutions that provide safety of principle and guaranteed retirement income streams. When Ryan talks about ROI, he means "Reliability of Income."

Ryan's harrowing journey into and slow burn out of a hell of multiple addictions is living proof that with deep faith, the encouragement of loving friends, sponsors, mentors and family, and an effective 12-step program, anything is possible. Taking full advantage of his second chance at life, he continues to build a successful business with hundreds of loyal clients while paying his reversal of fortune forward in many inspiring ways—including counseling those enrolled in a drug program at the Middlesex House of Corrections in Billerica and helping young students at his high school alma mater and other schools throughout his home region.

Summit Financial Partners' approach to working with clients is one that is both relaxed and confident. Our sound and well-researched solutions provide clients with solid financial plans. His areas of particular focus include: preserving and protecting client assets to ensure financial independence; determining how to maximize Social Security and other retirement benefits to provide maximum retirement income; and developing advantageous strategies for estate planning and asset distribution.

"My ultimate aim for every client relationships I have is that I provide peace, so they can sleep without any worry about having enough money to live on and enjoy their lives with," Ryan says. "My many years in the financial industry have taught me one essential truth: at the end of the day, all people want is someone who is honest and who genuinely cares."